ADULT RELIGIOUS EDUCATION

A Journey of Faith Development

by
**Marie A. Gillen
Maurice C. Taylor
Editors**

**Paulist Press
New York, Mahwah**

Library of Congress Cataloging–in–Publication Data

Adult religious education : a journey of faith development / by Marie
A. Gillen, Maurice C. Taylor, editors.
    p.   cm.
  Includes bibliographical references (p.   )
  ISBN 0-8091-3591-4 (alk. paper)
  1. Christian education of adults. 2. Catholic Church—Education.
I. Gillen, Marie A. II. Taylor, Maurice C.
BX921.A383   1995
268′.434—dc20

95-4701
CIP

Published by Paulist Press
997 Macarthur Boulevard
Mahwah, NJ 07430

Printed and bound in the
United States of America

CONTENTS

iii

105432

INTRODUCTION

The word journey usually conjures up ideas like making plans, seeking advice from travel agents or automobile clubs, asking others about their experiences, reflecting on past experiences as a journeyer and deciding what to bring and what to wear. A journey implies progress or passage from one place to another. The preparation stage is usually characterized by readiness: seeking out material and human resources, making up one's mind, putting things in order. The journey itself is a passage. It usually has a number of stages or phases. A successful journey is usually based on a combination of knowledge, understanding, attitudes and skills; that is, a solid sense of where one will be heading and the knack of applying this information to one's everyday experience of being on the journey.

The word journey in the title of this book is a fitting metaphor for what the book is all about. In brief, it is about adult faith development which is part of the lifelong learning journey. Words and phrases associated with journey, such as passage, progress, excursion, explorer, and planning a tour, fit very nicely with the various sections of this book. Each section is different, but the overriding theme in all is that adult religious education is part of a learning journey that requires serious consideration and cannot be taken for granted. The journey itself is facilitated by improving the practice of those engaged in adult religious education. The book dispels the notion that anyone can teach adult religious education. It points out that being well-grounded in dogma, rules and the Bible is not enough to be a good adult religious educator. It makes the point that all who are engaged in adult religious education are both teacher and learner at the same time. It is a lifelong learning process for everyone.

In this book, the editors have tried to capture something of the rich experience of adult religious educators by inviting a wide range of practitioners and analysts to

1

share their expertise and ideas on three major topics relating to adult faith development. Contributors include academics, clergy, adult education trainers, a learning mangager, a marriage and family counselor, lay ministers with family responsibilities, and a married woman with three young children.

WHAT'S THIS BOOK ALL ABOUT?

In Part I, *Understanding the Need for Adult Religious Education*, each chapter provides a personal interpretation of the need for adult religious education. This section advocates responding to the needs of learners while at the same time encouraging them to analyze assumptions, challenge previously accepted beliefs and values, and consider alternatives. Thus the central theme of this section is balance; that is, religious education is more than transmitting dogma and rules and studying the Bible. This is not enough; connection to everyday living and how people can become involved in contemporary problems has to be pointed out. Each chapter in this section provides a personal interpretation of the need for adult religious education.

In Part II, *The Many Dimensions of Adult Religious Education in the Community*, the reader becomes aware of the magnitude and greatness of the field as it relates to community. Magnitude is presented in light of responsiveness through the art and science of program planning and by a strong argument favoring critical thinking as a way of advancing the affective and spiritual dimensions of liturgical experience. Greatness is underscored by illustrating the importance of cultural factors in any community, and by proposing pastoral counseling as a unifying force within a community. Community responsiveness provides the rhythm for the journey in this section. It is grounded in the belief that there must always be an aspect of faith that is communal.

In Part III, *Improving Practice in Adult Religious*

Education, some tantalizing questions that beg for answers are dealt with. How does one become an effective adult religious educator? What are the many things that sustain an adult educator? Are there any new approaches for encouraging adults on their faith journey? How do issues like authenticity and ethics link to practice in adult religious education? In reading this section the reader realizes that improving practice is a complex issue. It must respect adult learners and must suit their faith development needs.

Any attempt to bring together a collection of writings on a new subject has its limitations. Such is the case with this book; it is not inclusive. It does not purport to represent all current views or practices relating to adult religious education but does try to capture a "snapshot" of the field. It is important to mention here that this specialized field is rich in expertise, but due to constraints all of these experts could not be invited to write under one cover.

There are a number of similar concepts and ideas found in some of the chapters. Several of them refer to the role of the facilitator, lifelong learning, adult educational principles, planning frameworks for adult religious education, methods and approaches to adult learning, and learning styles. We view these repetitive concepts and ideas as being a strengthening factor of the book. They demonstrate unity in a field that is diverse by its very nature. In some chapters the word church is capitalized; in others it isn't. The reason for this difference is specificity of the term. When a particular church is referred to the word is capitalized. Similarities and differences, such as those noted in this book, are the hallmark of adult religious education.

WHO COULD BENEFIT FROM READING THIS BOOK?

This book was written with a number of people in mind. The broad spectrum of writers who contributed to this book reflect this diversity: leaders, both lay and clerical; those who work in the ministry of adult religious education, both full-time and part-time; those who work in other ministries that make use of educational strategies; academics who have an interest in adult learning related to faith development; students of adult education who have an interest in this specialization, counselors; consultants with an interest in facilitation; and everyone with an interest in spiritual growth and development and how this might be facilitated. The list could go on. The point is that the intended readership is wide.

HOW SHOULD THIS BOOK BE READ?

As with most edited books you might not want to read it from cover to cover like a novel. Instead, we invite you to pick and choose. Readers should look through the table of contents first to get a general overview of the parts and the various chapters in each part. The next step would be to read the introduction to each part. This section provides a thumbnail sketch of each chapter and highlights its main points. Brief sketches about the authors are found at the end of each chapter, and also a set of questions. These questions vary depending on the nature of the chapter. Some questions serve as departure points for further reflection while others are intended to be practical guides for engaging others in the topic.

Keep in mind that this book is intended as a learning journey, as an adventure. Every chapter includes a learning challenge. For some it will be knowledge and understanding; for others it will be skills development, change of attitudes, or values clarification. Make the book work for you. Happy journeying!

ACKNOWLEDGEMENTS

We would like to express our gratitude to all the individual authors who labored so diligently and patiently to turn out this book. Their experiences and untiring efforts have helped in shaping the mosaic called adult religious education. Special appreciation and acknowledgment to John Reigle for his editing assistance. Our sincere thanks to Angela Stewart, St. Francis Xavier University, Antigonish, NS, and to the secretarial staff of the Faculty of Education, University of Ottawa, for their invaluable word processing skills.

PART I

UNDERSTANDING THE NEED
FOR ADULT RELIGIOUS EDUCATION

The concept of need has many different meanings; educational needs are no different. Educational needs generally fall into two categories: felt needs, that is, learners' expressions of preference or desire and prescribed needs, educators' beliefs about what they feel adults should acquire. The main theme in this section is not an either/or; it presents a balanced view that advocates responding to the needs of learners while at the same time encouraging them to analyze assumptions, challenge previously accepted beliefs and values, and consider alternatives. Other connecting themes in this section are: learning is a lifelong journey and reflection is the key to meaningful learning. This section attempts to articulate the need for adult religious education more clearly and to set the stage for the other sections that follow.

The question of what it means to develop one's faith is a significant one; it is pivotal to understanding the need for adult religious education. In the first chapter Marie Gillen makes the case that religious education is never the transmission of faith for its own sake. Its purpose is to enable persons to have a personal relationship with God. Her major conclusion is that one way this can be done effectively is by utilizing the significant events of the decade to broaden the context for faith development. Her discussion begins with the very basic concept that adults learn differently and that these differences have implications for learning. She proposes experiential learning as being particularly relevant for learning from the events of the last decade and for adult faith development in general. Learning from these events as a vehicle for faith

7

development calls for making meaning from these events in terms of one's spiritual well-being. Gillen points out that this requires an organic connection between what is going on in the world, what is happening with the learner, as well as a number of other variables.

In chapter 2, Remi De Roo tells us that life is filled with assumptions, one of these being that the church is indeed a forum for adult religious education. His point in this chapter is that the role of adult religious education is to help adults realize that the bodies of knowledge, accepted truths, commonly held values, and customary behaviors comprising their worlds are contextually and culturally constructed. Through being prompted to consider alternative ideas and values, adults can come to an awareness of the essential contingencies of their worlds with respect to their faith. Such an awareness in his view is the necessary prelude to their taking action to alter their personal and collective circumstances. De Roo's ideas are brought together in his description of the synod gathering in his own diocese.

In chapter 3, Caryl Green makes the point that the church has a responsibility to challenge us to grow beyond our blind spots and our points of denial. She then begs the questions: Is the church the place where adults can risk and ask questions, especially if these questions challenge the established truth? Is the church a place where adults experience love and respect? In her chapter Green explains what she calls freedoms for growth. She very skilfully presents three stories of faith development. She concludes that the need for adult religious education is based on the belief that faith is not meant to remain at a personal level. There must always be an aspect of faith that reaches out to others, that is communal.

Margaret Fisher Brillinger, in chapter 4, expands the view of faith development from something that is done to the learner in the classroom setting to a daily ongoing journey of discovery and meaning-making. She points out that adult learning in a religious context is more than simply ongoing learning of religious information and perspectives. It includes the development of adults as spiritual people. Other issues explored in this chapter that contribute to the understanding for the need for adult religious education include holistic learning, learning as transformation, educational principles and their implications, and the contributions of adult religious learning to adult development in general.

The main thrust in this section is that adults, as well as children, are now involved in religious education: no longer does what was learned in youth prepare one for her or his Christian role in life. By clearly understanding the need for adult religious education, religious leaders and educators can build a foundation for practising more effectively.

1. LEARNING FROM THE SIGNIFICANT EVENTS OF THE DECADE

Marie A. Gillen

Much has happened in the last decade. The dissolution of the Soviet Empire, the Gulf Crisis, the Chernobyl reactor disintegration and the dizzying advances in the use of technology are some of these occurrences. Other, less newsworthy but equally significant events or phenomena include peace marches, the signing of the North America Free Trade Agreement, the recession, and changes in the definition of family. These events are not simply interesting or exciting material for the media or for scientific reflection; they are events that can provide data from which ordinary people can learn about their roles in and perspectives on society.

Events can be looked at in different ways. They might be viewed as anything that happens or is regarded as happening: an occurrence—especially one of some importance. The Gulf Crisis, for example, is an event that undeniably happened. During this period North Americans were bombarded day and night by media reports while Iraqis were simply bombarded. Apprehension enveloped most of the world and there was a general sigh of relief, amidst the hoopla, when it was all over. Technology is different. Advances in technology are regarded as happening continuously, and are recognized even by the most uninvolved. The impact of technological advances is inescapable. A trip to the local supermarket these days puts one in touch with scanner check-out systems; weekly banking has been impersonalized by automatic tellers.

Another way of viewing events is by way of the outcome or the consequences. One outcome of the collapse of the giant Soviet Union in 1991, for example, is a rising class of hustlers emerging in the land of Lenin amid the poor and hungry. As a nation of 145 million people struggles to make the transition from totalitarianism to democracy, there are many conflicting social, political, and economic strains. The majority in Russia are struggling to survive inflation-ravaged incomes, while others are becoming rich and infamous. Similarly, for Chernobyl, the consequences in the aftermath of this disaster is that about 8,000 people have died from radiation-induced diseases caused by the accident. The chain of cause and effect goes on and on.[1]

This chapter offers a new way of thinking about what it means to develop one's faith by utilizing the significant events of the decade to broaden the context of faith development. It is intended to promote thinking and reflection about appropriate learning approaches and offers a few practical suggestions. It stresses that adult religious education is more than transmitting dogma and rules. It is a more dynamic whole that calls for a new definition and a new agenda for the future. More than ever in recent history, adults are reconsidering their religious understanding. The churches and community groups need to reconsider appropriate approaches to promote adult religious learning. Consequently, the questions that arise for this chapter are: How does one learn from these events, and how does this learning connect with faith development? These questions raise some tantalizing issues. Before they can be examined, however, another question begs for an answer: How do adults learn?

As a prelude to answering this question, and as a background for understanding faith development better, we as educators should reflect on a very basic concept: adults learn differently; they do not all learn the same way. Like physical differences in people, there are learning differences, too. The nice thing about learning differences is that there is no right or wrong way. Each person develops her or his personal repertoire of approaches to new learning. What and how one learns differs according to whether the learning is theoretical or practical—studying a car manual or getting under the hood to fix the car, according to whether the concepts involved are ideal or real—something that exists in the imagination or something that actually is happening, and so on. Each of these differences has some implications for learning.

HOW ADULTS LEARN

Any attempt to define adult learning presupposes philosophical questions. How knowledge is related to experience is undoubtedly a philosophical question. Similarly, how educators understand the way in which knowledge arises out of experience involves one's philosophical perspective. When one is faced with questions such as, "How do people learn things?" and "How do people acquire an understanding of things?" the only general answer that is possible is, "In all sorts of ways." How people learn depends on who and where they are, and where they start from in the learning process. For example, an engineer might learn about a new type of machinery by drawing or studying diagrams, whereas a mechanic might learn about new machinery by examining a prototype or by a hands-on approach—that is, working with the machine directly.

A Variety of Factors

It is certainly not enough to present a person with a wide range of experiences and expect the person to learn unless he or she is in the position to attend to these learning experiences. There are a number of factors that need to be considered in learning, not all of which need bear solely on intellectual considerations. There are also emotional and motivational considerations. There are, moreover, social considerations which may affect the kind of environment in which the individual grows up and lives, and the opportunities that this affords or stunts. There are, no doubt, other considerations that arise from the individual's own make-up, character, personality, and temperament.

Learning from experience is commonly called experiential learning. It is not the only way to learn, but this approach has captured the interest of adult educators because of its relevance for the adult learner. Experiential learning is an important focus in any discussion about learning from the significant events of the decade.

Experiential Learning—What Is It?

Experiential learning is deeply rooted in the ideas of John Dewey,[2] who broadened the view of education. He understood education to be a lifelong process, which includes the concept that learners have personal needs, interests, experiences, and desires. He refuted the "empty vessel" notion of the liberal orientation to learning and considered the school simply as one agency among many responsible for learning. In his view learning takes place in many institutions of society, such as churches, family, and the workplace. He anchored his thinking on the assumption of an organic connection between education and personal experience. Dewey's ideas have broad applicability to the field of adult education and have greatly influenced other forms of education and learning. Mary Boys says that Dewey contributed to religious education by providing "religious educators with the impetus to use the social sciences and to incorporate psychology into their considerations; it legitimized their awakening sense of the dual character of education as both a political activity and a religious act."[3]

David Kolb offers a working definition of experiential learning: "Learning is the process whereby knowledge is created through the transformation of experience."[4] He explains four important aspects of experiential learning: (a) the emphasis is on the process of learning rather than content or outcome; (b) knowledge is transformative; it is continuously being created and re-created; it is not a set of dictums to be merely transmitted; (c) learning changes people's perspectives about their new experiences; and (d) the process of learning is tied to the notion of knowledge, and to understand either one requires understanding the other.[5]

Peter Jarvis argues that Kolb's definition is restrictive and offers a more inclusive one in which he adds skills and attitudes to the notion of knowledge. Jarvis says that "life is about experience, wherever there is life there are potential learning experiences."[6] Jarvis and Kolb, however, agree on one fundamental point, which Jarvis calls "the centrality of the idea of reflection."[7] As they see it reflection is important because it helps adults break out of the learning boundaries set by society. Ironically, by so doing, they expand not only their intellectual and spiritual boundaries, but also their economic and social possibilities. Reflection assists adults in making the transition from being passive learners, who accept the limitations of what is provided by others without testing the truth of what is being said, to becoming active learners able to define meanings and gain new perspectives on their own. Like Martin Luther King, who had a dream, they too have a dream, one that provides goals and sires purpose.

LEARNING BY EXPERIENCE

Some general learnings are fairly obvious. In the case of industrial disasters like Chernobyl, the most likely learning by ordinary people is a greater regard for safety and the environment. This often translates into citizens taking action when a government proposes to set up a new industrial facility, such as an incinerator to burn toxic waste near where one lives, or into taking part in a writing campaign on some environmental issue. For technological advances, most people learn to live with changes. We are surrounded by modern wonders to make life easier and more rewarding—vacuum cleaner, washer and dryer, microwave oven, remote controlled television, VCR, stereo, and answering machine. Technology was supposed to relieve people of the drudgery of everyday living and to make us happier. One problem which is borne out by personal experience is that technology accelerates the pace of life by letting us do things faster and easier. Technology seduces with its glitter and obvious benefits. At the very time that we should be slowing down and pulling back, technology draws us in the opposite direction.

Other learnings are debatable, and some might convincingly argue that human beings never learn from some of life's events, war being one of these. If they did, why do wars continue today? What did the world learn from World War I besides the fact that wars could no longer be fought on the ground alone, but that the control of air space would be essential as well. The world obviously failed to learn the important lesson that war is not the answer, that many lives are lost needlessly, that those who live through the onslaught suffer untold misery and grief, and that peace should be pursued at any cost. If the world had learned, World War I really would have been the war to end all wars. Instead, we had World War II, and in this decade the Gulf Crisis, the many conflicts in Eastern Europe and the Middle East, and the many other skirmishes of the last decade, such as the war in Somalia. So let it be said, based on the evidence of history, that people throughout the world have not learned anything positive from the horrors of war over the years.

Violence is going on all over the world even as one reads this page. Radio and television blare out these events almost daily, and dramatic newspaper headlines bring to the notice of the public the stark reality of the latest violent happening. The ills of violence and prejudice are displayed daily on every newscast. The influence of the media in shaping people's attitudes and values toward violence remains often unnoticed but nevertheless very great. One way of overcoming this influence is education, because violence is born of prejudice, of lack of understanding, of lack of communication. Education is the most potent remedy to war and violence, the best and perhaps only effective measure we know. It breaks down walls of isolation and ignorance, seeks solutions to problems, and leads to peace and understanding.

Adult learners are good at making sense of their experiences. They all have to start with what they have been given and to operate within horizons set by ways of seeing and understanding that have been shaped by language, culture and personal experience, which they have acquired through prior learning. For this reason learning from the significant events of a decade is something like putting together a jigsaw puzzle—there are many pieces that all fit together. However, there is a difference. Just as you think you've got it, the picture keeps changing. And suddenly, the old pieces no longer fit the new picture, even though they seem to slip into place. For example, issues pertaining to human sexuality have been compounded during this past decade by the new epidemic of the 1980s: AIDS. At times learning is a bit like putting together pieces of jelly to create a picture of the world. The world keeps changing as if the pieces of jelly were melting. But people need a good picture of the world, in order to know where they stand and how they should interrelate with it and each other. Thus, even though the pieces keep changing, it is important for a person to keep putting the picture together in order to establish a meaningful perspective.

The jigsaw puzzle is a fitting metaphor for many aspects of learning from the events of the decade because it supports the notion that knowledge is continually being created and re-created. Looking back over the decade's various events and developments, one is struck again and again by how much life is characterized by the manifold pieces of modern everyday life. The question is not whether one will learn from the experiences of the past decade but rather how one sorts out the pieces. It is also a question of how one matches up the colors of the puzzle pieces, and how well one is able to stick with the task of putting the pieces together—an essential process in getting at the bigger picture—and of making sense out of it, then using this learning to propel oneself forward in a positive way. One positive direction is one way of linking learning to one's faith. It is a process of looking for similarities and differences between present and prior learning challenges, drawing conclusions, and seeking ways to express ideas and to create metaphors that enrich learning.

The metaphor of growth is an essential part of our image of the adult. This is not just a fanciful and unfounded idea, but one that gives meaning to the notion of adult faith development. We know that adults are vulnerable and imperfect, but we also know that they have a rich life experience which, properly tapped, will strengthen their personal meaning system by refocusing or extending their expectations about how things are supposed to be. As Paul-André Giguere points out, "Human beings cannot reach their full potential unless they enter into social and communal relationship with others. God's plan of salvation is one of communion and solidarity,"[8] which in turn strives for inspiration and perfection in all domains of knowledge and creation.

The broader circumstances in which people act—that is, the significant events that surround them—must now be looked at; these circumstances are, in many ways, different from others before. The picture keeps changing almost daily. Therefore, in order for adult religious education to be relevant, "content needs to emerge from the needs and questions experienced and expressed by persons and by the community as they relate to others and to the environment."[9] A good example is the influence of the media. It shapes attitudes and values in subtle ways, but the sway is immense.

LINK WITH ADULT FAITH DEVELOPMENT

Recognition of and the need to enhance religious educational opportunities across age levels has been one of the great advances in church circles during the last decade. The historical tradition had been that religious education was a task for the young, occupying a particular time in life, with a beginning and an end. This idea perpetuated the notion that adults either could not learn or did not need to learn, physically or intellectually, after a certain level of maturation. Today there is more emphasis on and a new interest in religious education for adults rather than simply the familiar nurturing of children and youth. This is very positive and fits very well with learning, an idea that places the adult learner in the context of the learning society. Lifelong learning is one way of overcoming the separation that exists between life and living. The phenomenon dispels the erroneous opinion that the formal educational system is the only place where learning happens. If faith development is to be a lifelong learning process, religious education requires a different approach; it needs to be understood within the context of everyday experience.

The idea that religion can be divided into neat intellectual categories is governed by an educational philosophy that is no longer relevant today. Reason can no longer be separated from emotion, and self from the other, without tragic consequences. The human being can no longer be governed by the head alone; the heart, hands, body and spirit are needed as well. For example, dogmatic sermons are not enough; the connections to everyday living and how people can become involved in contemporary problems has to be pointed out. Without these pieces fitting together the jigsaw puzzle will never form a proper picture. Going back to the metaphor of the jigsaw puzzle might be a good place to start in examining how experiential learning can be used in adult faith development, because one aspect of this approach is that knowledge is transformative.

Adult religious education should begin with questions relating to issues like unemployment, ethics, and economics. What have faith communities to say about such issues? These questions and many others are all pieces of the jigsaw puzzle, and beg the further question: How can religion be taught if one doesn't start from the experiences of life? The gospel of Matthew (17:1-9) provides a good example. Jesus and the disciples are on their way to Jerusalem. While on the mountain top, Jesus' face shines "like the sun." Moses and Elijah appear and speak with him; God also appears saying, "This is my Son, the Beloved." Faced with all of this Peter wants to remain in the presence of the holy ones. But Jesus knows that they cannot stay; they must continue their journey, and he must suffer and die on the cross to witness to God's saving power. So, they move on. This is a good example of being taught from the experience of life. Peter got caught up in the moment; he wanted to bask forever in the vision. Jesus reminded the disciples of reality; life goes on. They were on a journey. They must learn from the experience of moving on, not from standing still. Where there is a vision, the tourist becomes a pilgrim, and the bystander becomes a wayfarer. The world keeps changing. It is a process of understanding the relationship to one another and to a common experience. It is a process of struggling with the pieces of the puzzle that make up one's world.

Donald Emler argues, "It is a goal of religious education to enable persons to have a personal relationship with God. It is never the transmission of facts for their own sake."[10] The objective is not a set of dictums to be merely transmitted. As with the example of Jesus and the disciples on the way to Jerusalem, along the way we encounter people of faith; we are given signs that reveal God's love for us. The simple transmission of facts rarely prompts people to apply religious concepts to their own lives or to have a personal relationship with God, because the connection of facts to everyday experience somehow falls between the cracks and gets lost. People do not seem to be on the right wavelength, they are not getting the message.

Take for example the passage from John's gospel in which Jesus is talking to the Pharisees. He said:

> I tell you most solemnly, anyone who does not
> enter the sheepfold through the gate, but gets in
> some other way is a thief and a brigand. The one
> who enters by the gate is the shepherd of the
> flock; the gatekeeper lets him in, the sheep hear
> his voice, one by one he calls his own sheep and
> leads them out. When he has brought out all his
> flock, he goes ahead of them, and the sheep
> follow him because they know his voice. They
> will not follow a stranger, but they will run from
> him: they do not recognize the voice of strangers
> (John 10:1-5).

When Jesus told this story, his listeners, the Pharisees,
failed to understand what he meant, so he told the story
again, in a slightly different way.

> I tell you most solemnly, I am the gate for the
> sheepfold. All others who have come are thieves
> and brigands; but the sheep took no notice of
> them. I am the gate. Anyone who enters through
> me will be safe. He will go freely in and go out and
> be sure of finding pasture. The thief comes only
> to steal and kill and destroy. I have come so that
> they may have life and have it to the full (John
> 10:7-10).

Jesus' hearers still did not understand; the messages
seemed unclear. The reason was that the story emphasized
the process of learning rather than the content or
outcome. The Pharisees, in listening to Jesus, understood
his message in terms of content—shepherds and the sheep;
they failed to hear the deeper message of conditions to be
true followers of Christ. Jesus was telling them that they
must not only become like him, but must act like him;
there is no room for pretending. They would have to be
authentic, otherwise people would see through them and
stop listening altogether. The Pharisees were confused; the
message was not easy to understand because they were

sanctimonious, self-righteous, and hypocritical persons who advocated strict observance of external forms of conduct and religion without regard to the spirit.

There is much evidence to support the assertion that one tends to accept and integrate experiences that comfortably fit one's frame of reference and to discount those that do not. Jesus' story did not make sense to the Pharisees, because they were not able to relate it to their past experience. Perhaps they did not know what trustworthy was and what it meant to be reliable or authentic. Increased understanding of the world comes about through a knowledge or understanding involved in having concepts, given certain background conditions. In the case of the Pharisees these ideas did not fit. The same is true today, and unless one experiences a concrete community experience of deeply felt acceptance and care the experience will have no meaning. A focus on God's unconditional love and a call to fellowship is not enough. Giguere says, "It is in real life that the call to discipleship is received and the response given."[11] The call lifts one above the commonplace with assurances of greater things to come. It gives significance to even the drudgeries of life because no chore, however menial it may appear, is meaningless within the context of discipleship.

Beginning with life's experiences often leads people to the position of finding truth from within—that is, learning by living. This assertion raises the question of interpreting experience. Are all experiences significant? The answer is, quite simply, no. There are what Jarvis (1987) calls "meaningful and meaningless experiences."[12]

MEANINGFUL AND MEANINGLESS EXPERIENCES

In everyday life, people go about their daily tasks in a rather automatic manner. They eat, sleep, go to work, and enjoy the company of family and friends in an almost unthinking manner. Take, for instance, the simple task of brushing one's teeth. The act of brushing one's teeth is so meaningful that it can be taken for granted. People's knowledge base is sufficient to carry out this meaningful task many times daily in an automatic way. But what about times when the knowledge from daily living is not able to provide an automatic response—in other words, the situation is no longer a taken for granted? This is often the case when some financial risk is involved. Jarvis says, "When there is disjunction between individuals' own biography and the socio-cultural-temporal world of their experience, then a potential learning experience has occurred."[13] In other words, a person being strongly influenced on the one hand by the external force of media to buy something, and on the other hand by the values and attitudes instilled during youth which cautioned against living beyond one's means.

The key words here are disjunction and potential. The word disjunction means separation, disconnection, isolation, severance. This is often the case with displaced workers who find themselves in a retraining program. They generally experience a great deal of social anxiety and dislocation. The impact of isolation can be severe on esteem and mental health. Displaced workers often become distrustful. However, once involved in a community-based training program they generally respond to supportive staff and the opportunity to interact with others in similar circumstances, and their self-esteem grows. Thus, the possibility of meaningful learning increases.

If the disjunction is extreme, if it is too great, the experience will be meaningless. People withdraw, they become disaffected and turn away. This was the case after Vatican II in the Catholic Church when the disjunction caused by the implementation of the documents was in some cases simply too disjunctive. Ideas were foisted on people without any explanation. Many were heard to say, "What is going on?" "Why do I feel that this is no longer my church?" Dewey refers to similar experiences as "miseducative"; he says, "any experience is miseducative that has the effect of arresting or distorting the growth of further experience."[14] In the case of Vatican II, many people's prior knowledge was inadequate for them to handle the experience of the many changes in the church. Their faith development was arrested because the new experiences they were having were meaningless in terms of their previous experiences.

The handling of disjunction is the role of the adult religious educator, broadly defined. This role is often described by the term *facilitator* rather than teacher. This function implies "presenting alternatives, questioning givens, and scrutinizing the self," which is different from the kind of teaching in which children are the learners.[15] A facilitator is like a tight-rope walker, straddling the fine line between meaningful and meaningless learning. A facilitator can help people to keep putting the picture of the world together like in a jigsaw puzzle so that they can link what is going on around them with their faith. How and whether the experience is a meaningful one depends on, among other things, what the person takes the experience as, what the experience means to the person, and whether—for a variety of reasons, not all of which are intellectual—the experience is capable of meaning anything to the person. A facilitator's role is difficult to assess because success is difficult to measure. How can one ascertain the value of a few words which can move people to do good or evil, to reach out or to reject others, to see things in new ways or to remain stagnant?

THE HANDLING OF DISJUNCTION

The key to success in handling disjunction is reflection. Reflection is an essential phase in the learning process. It often makes the difference between a disjunction becoming a meaningful or a meaningless experience. It is a way to make sense out of one's experience and to use these insights to make decisions or to take action. An example may clarify this process.

Consider a group that is discussing one of the significant events of this decade, the amassing of multi-million dollar deficits in developed and developing countries. Disjunction might be the feeling of separation and disconnection from this problem; it has not touched the participants' lives. Or, the participants might fall into the trap of being blinded by the truly difficult financial times in which they live or by the facts of unemployment and inflation instead of focusing on the real purpose of the session, which is faith development. A skilled facilitator could bring the group through a reflective process which would invite the participants to look critically at their personal lives in comparison to the condition of the world in which they live. The context for this might be Deuteronomony, where Moses said to the people: "I set before you life or death, blessing or curse. Choose life, then, so that you and your descendants may live" (Deuteronomony 30:19).

The important question becomes: why and how have persons, regions, countries, and sometimes whole continents ended up in the disastrous situation in which they now are? The answer Moses would have given is that in the practical choices of their lives, humanity failed to take life itself as the most important issue. Instead of human life they chose other things: property, money, esteem, honor. They sacrificed their lives and the lives of countless others to their greed. Participants can be invited to reflect for a few minutes on their own agenda. Is that agenda a choice for life in God's way? Do their choices help others to live? Do they allow others to flourish? Reminded by the fact that Christians are urged to read the signs of the times and to strengthen, support, and celebrate all that gives hope in the future, the participants might be urged to formulate some steps for action. These could take a number of forms: further reflection, prayer, getting involved with a local action group, extending oneself to someone in need. The options are endless. The point of the action is to connect human beings with God's plan of salvation, which is one of communion and solidarity.

The action has issued from the needs and questions experienced by persons and by the community as they relate to others and to the environment. This is what faith development is all about. It is helping people to put the jigsaw puzzle of life together today, fully aware that it probably will change tomorrow. But building today helps them to build a better tomorrow.

SIGNIFICANCE FOR THE CONTEMPORARY CHURCH OF LEARNING FROM EVENTS

This discussion of how one learns from the events of the past decade and of ways to connect this learning with one's faith development began with the very basic concept that adults learn differently and that these differences have implications for learning. The experiential learning approach was proposed as being particularly relevant for this type of learning. Some learnings are obvious; others are debatable. The metaphor of the jigsaw puzzle was woven throughout the chapter and was used to explain the learning process and the links with adult faith development. Examples from the scriptures illustrated key points.

There are differences between meaningful and meaningless experiences. Reflection is an important process that can help experiences become meaningful. Learning from the events of the past decade as a vehicle for faith development calls for making meaning from these events in terms of one's own spiritual well-being. This requires an organic connection between what is going on in the world, one's personal experiences, God's plan of salvation, and the contemporary church structure.

DISCUSSION QUESTIONS

1. Think back on past learning experiences. Pick out one experience that inspired you; pick out another that had the opposite effect. How do you account for the difference in the two experiences? How do you learn best?

2. What particular events of the past decade have caused you to pause and reflect? Why were these events meaningful? How did you handle any disjunction?

3. As a facilitator of adult learning how can you assist others to connect what is going on around them with their faith? Draw on your personal faith development learning journey, and also consider other people's various learning styles.

NOTES

1. The events used illustratively in this chapter have been drawn from a variety of sources. All have been widely reported by newspapers, television journalists, and news journals. The weekly magazines, such as *Time* and *Newsweek*, are useful sources for researching significant current events.

2. John Dewey's ideas have laid the foundations for many current ideas about adult education and about learning from experience. See John Dewey, *Democracy and Education* (New York: Macmillan, 1916) and John Dewey, *Experience and Education* (New York: Macmillan, 1938).

3. Mary C. Boys, *Educating in Faith: Maps and Vision* (San Francisco: Harper & Row, 1987), p.49.

4. David A. Kolb, *Experiential Learning: Experience as the Source of Learning and Development* (Englewood Cliffs, N.J.: Prentice-Hall, 1984), p. 360.

5. Ibid., Kolb provides a philosophical and theoretical rationale for experiential learning by drawing upon a wide variety of disciplines and theories.

6. Peter C. Jarvis, "Meaningful and Meaningless Experience: Toward an Analysis of Learning from Life," *Adult Education Quarterly* 37, no.3 (Spring, 1987), p.164.

7. Ibid., p. 165.

8. Paul-André Giguere (ed.), "Christian Orientation in

Adult Education: A Synthesis of Our Vision," *Insight: A Resource for Adult Religious Education, no.2* (1988), p. 8. (An annual publication of Canadian Conference of Catholic Bishops, Ottawa, ON.) This article presents Christian adult education from three perspectives: the image of the person, the main orientation of Christian adult education, and the content of Christian adult education.

9. Ibid., p. 14.

10. Donald G. Emler, *Revisioning the DRE* (Birmingham, Ala: Religious Education Press, 1989), p. 241.

11. Giguere, "Christian Orientation in Adult Education," p. 12.

12. Jarvis, "Meaningful and Meaningless Experience," p. 167.

13. Ibid., p. 168.

14. Dewey, *Experience and Education*, p. 25.

15. Stephen D. Brookfield, *Understanding and Facilitating Adult Learning* (San Francisco: Jossey-Bass, 1986), p. 125.

ABOUT THE AUTHOR

Marie A. Gillen is Professor of Adult Education at St. Francis Xavier University, Antigonish, Nova Scotia. She holds a masters degree in Church History from the Catholic University of America in Washington, D.C. and a doctorate in educational theory with a specialization in adult education from the University of Toronto. She has been a consultant to the National Office of Religious Education, the Canadian Conference of Catholic Bishops and was principal investigator for their recently released research project: *Pathways to Faithfulness: Developing Structures Which Support Catechetical Ministry with Adults.* She has written a number of articles on adult religious education. Marie is a member of the Sisters of Charity, Halifax.

2. THE CHURCH AS A CONTEMPORARY STRUCTURE FOR ADULT RELIGIOUS EDUCATION

Remi J. De Roo

Some time ago I was on a trip to Brazil to participate in an Ecumenical Encounter of church leaders. Arriving at the conference registration desk, I noticed my name was written incorrectly. Assuming that someone had made a mistake, I corrected it, picked up my kit and gave this incident no further thought. Shortly after, a vivacious woman approached me. How surprised she was to discover I was a man, as she had been informed a woman from Canada would share her room!

The routine of daily life is filled with assumptions. People take so many things for granted. Identifying assumptions about church, society, government, family and other institutions might result in animated discussions which challenge, disrupt, or motivate one to action.

This chapter identifies one of my assumptions: that the church is indeed a forum for adult religious education. The Catholic community has always valued an ongoing faith development. Models of education in which people learn from one another have evolved over the years. Witness the return of the Rite of Christian Initiation, social justice education, and scripture study. Moreover, based on contemporary research and practice, our faith community encourages and promotes the discovery of new ways to enrich one's faith journey. Identifying one's experience, reflecting on it in the light of gospel values, and gathering in information and wisdom fosters deeper living of one's faith. However, assumptions vary from one person to another, from one local church community to another. One's assumptions regarding society affect the style and the needs to which the church must lead or respond.

This chapter presents a wide variety of assumptions, suppositions and ideas about the church as a contemporary structure for adult religious education. These considerations sometimes seem almost like aphorisms. They are presented here to spur the adult religious educator to reflect upon his or her assumptions and ideas about a wide range of relevant topics. Frequent questions are interspersed to help promote that reflection. Near the end of the chapter, I provide an illustrative example of how one diocese used the experiences of parish members to contribute to the church's vision and direction as a contemporary structure for continuing faith development. The discussion questions at the end provide many further focal points for directed reflection.

Assumptions about Church

For some, the church is seen as a convenient entity which is there to take care of them when they need God. For others, it is primarily the concern of a group of priests and their bishop. For yet others, the church has all the answers. They simply feel called to listen and to live honest lives. Others experience church as a structure which is contemporary in its outlook. They see their community interested in the faith development of adults as well as of children. Contemporary faith issues are named and honored. Based on their assumptions, some folks take it for granted that the church as presently constituted is an effective structure for adult faith development.

Assumptions about Society

The first matter to consider is the society in which the church is immersed. How many people assume that the particular form of democracy most common today is the best that can be found? How many citizens trust that society will naturally take care of their basic needs? When problems present themselves, how many people assume there are really no alternatives, that they have no choice but to make the best of things? How often is the statement made that conditions today aren't really all that bad?

Yet, there is something seriously out of kilter in the world. Certain facts need to be acknowledged realistically. Space does not permit listing them here. At the same time, it is purposeless to emphasize only the negative factors. There are also positive aspects to the profound transitions we are experiencing.

This is an exciting period in which to be alive. It provides great opportunities. This providential time of transition challenges people to recognize that a new world seeks to be born. Like the world at large, the church too is in labor. Christian believers are struggling to give form to a renewed model of a faith community that can provide hope and inspiration for humankind.

Church Structure: Theocracy, Monarchy, Democracy, or What?

The theories of political science and sociology do not apply directly to ecclesial structures. Emerging out of the disciples' experience of the risen Christ, the inner reality of the church will always remain a mystery. It was not established as a ready-made or prefabricated entity. It grew out of a divine mission in contact with the various social, cultural, and political environments where the gospel was preached. Its purpose is to promote the reign of God. The church is not meant to be equated with a theocracy, a monarchy, a republic, a democracy, a deliberating circle, a special interest group, a worldly power, or any other secular structure. However, it has been shaped by human experience and is conditioned by history.

Church leadership needs to express itself through some visible form, because it is made up of human beings. There will always be room for adaptation and healthy compromise in the face of evolving reality. The church constantly learns as it teaches. Leaders can enrich their wisdom through their mistakes. Continual internal conversion is even more important that external reform or modernizing.

Prejudice Based on Assumptions

Church history reveals the dire consequences of biased assumptions. Why did so many Europeans who came to North America treat the Aboriginal peoples like a lesser form of human beings? Why were so many baptized under duress? Europeans were confident that they were a superior civilization. They assumed their expression of Christianity was the only appropriate one. There are twenty-two rites in communion with Rome. From whence comes this sense that one rite is better than another?

Agents of Change in Church and Society

Fidelity to its mission requires that the contemporary church constantly and consistently promote social change. A distinguished Methodist lay theologian from Uruguay, Dr. Julio de Santa Ana, was one of the speakers at the Encounter in Brazil. He demonstrated how the world economy is dominated today by a single globally structured system.

This kind of information needs to be given serious attention. Realistic solutions to problems of distributive justice must take into account the macrorealities (broader dimensions) and the cosmogenesis (creative evolution) from which the social order develops. Otherwise, proposals for change may prove to be unrealistic. A willingness to engage in lifelong learning is therefore required.

According to Dr. Julio, effective social transformation involves five interlocking steps, each one critically important. *One must begin by learning to learn. One then learns to analyze, to interpret, to communicate and to transform.* This demands verification of the facts about reality as it is, not as observers might wish it were. This requires serious structural analysis of the power relationships that have fashioned institutions and structures, consciously or otherwise, down through the centuries. It means striving toward a high degree of objectivity in interpreting the facts that are brought to light. It also involves communicating effectively with modern culture, in messages that really say what is meant.

It will not suffice for reformers to denounce the evils in society and to proclaim utopias. Unrealistic ideals can become illusions or ideological traps. Specific projects are needed, with lasting commitment to achieve them. It is equally essential to empower the victims of power struggles, individually and collectively, so that they can bring about realistic and lasting changes.

The Church and Education for Social Change

In recent years the Catholic bishops of North America have been critiquing social structures and advocating a variety of changes. For example, documents emanating from the Canadian Social Affairs Commission have proposed a methodology for social transformation. It involves a spiral process which begins with our identifying compassionately with the poor and the oppressed. It is essential to really listen to their stories. Their lived experiences provide keys to meaningful solutions. In solidarity with the victims of society, a structural analysis of reality must be undertaken in the light of revealed values and biblical principles. The procedure also requires the elaboration of creative alternatives to current problems and the empowerment of those who are presently powerless. They need to become subjects—that is, autonomous agents—who can help shape their own history. That entails the formation of grass roots movements and popular coalitions to address the political dynamics whereby institutions are transformed.

The question one may raise here is about what social change has to do with adult faith development. One answer is that lifelong education is both an imperative and a moral enterprise. Is church membership at large being called upon to become real subjects, that is people responsible for their own destiny? Are people kept fully informed about spiritual and moral issues and about the options open to them? Is the expression of personal and collective responsibility welcomed and facilitated? Are critical assessments of current church policies readily received? Are the faithful encouraged to hold their leaders fully accountable? The current widespread alienation among youth and adults may have a positive aspect. An awakening is occurring; it is manifest in a healthy resistance to leadership when the leadership is perceived as autocratic.

History shows that clerics have rendered great service to the Christian community. Their very dedication may have been one reason why they gradually came to exercise such tremendous power. However, centuries of clerical control have caused some distorted relationships. The Catholic Church has a relatively small fully committed membership. The great majority remain passive recipients of sacramental ministry. Vast numbers of people who consider themselves good Christians do not perceive evangelization as their personal responsibility. To what extent are church leaders prepared to admit that fact and to face its consequences? Radical renewal is required. This is the proper domain of adult faith formation.

Renewal Prompted by the Second Vatican Council

The Second Vatican Council reaffirmed some ancient traditions. It declared that on the basis of faith and baptism, all the members of Christ's body are truly equal in dignity and in capacity to serve. The Holy Spirit has endowed all believers with a variety of gifts or charisms for the proclamation of the gospel and the development of the church as the divinely constituted agent for proclaiming the Good News. God has been revealed in the person of Jesus Christ, incarnate, crucified, risen. In the power of his Spirit he remains the present One. The covenant made with Abraham and Sarah is now more clearly ordered toward its fulfillment. All humankind is invited to the banquet table in the realm of God. There is no distinction henceforth between Jew or Gentile, slave or free, woman or man. One could go on in this vein.

But what has really happened in the course of time? To what extent has the message of Jesus been distorted by the various cultures in which the gospel was proclaimed? Do we find his preferential option for the poor and the marginalized manifest everywhere in the church today?

Faith and Justice

The capitalist theory which has shaped the current global economic system is based on the ideology of accumulation and centralization of wealth and power. Issues of distributive justice are left to the providence of an "invisible hand." The system reluctantly grants to less fortunate people such limited concessions as prove necessary to maintain its monopoly control.

Capitalism has long promoted the ideology of possessive individualism, now deeply ingrained in our culture. Few people are scandalized when opulent neighbors flaunt their wealth next to indigent families. Some analysts see a major shift presently occurring in the world market system. Increasingly centralized, it appears to be moving into new arenas where capital can increase its domination over labor. The global economic system appears to be in crisis everywhere, and no obvious solutions seem in store. It is not easy to discern what shape the future will take. Another dimension of this economic dilemma is the growing number of people who are marginalized by the competitive market system. They survive with difficulty in what has come to be known as the "informal economy." Most of these people live in what is called the "poor South" as compared with the "rich North." However, pockets of destitute people are also multiplying in affluent northern countries. People to whom one can apply a very simple image: those who are unable to carry credit cards. From a capitalist market economy perspective, they are treated as insignificant, ultimately expendable. Entire nations may eventually be sacrificed to the idols of greed, wealth, and power. These partial insights form an important background for reflecting on the role of adult believers in contemporary society. The majority of Christians will soon be living among the poorer peoples of the world.

The church has an unprecedented challenge to help direct humankind toward a destiny shaped by justice enlivened by compassion. Biblical tradition from its inception indicates that theology drew its main inspiration from God's presence among and solidarity with the poor. Church members are challenged to move beyond the current obsession with parish structures and internal power. They have a more important pastoral mission in the sphere of temporal activity and social transformation. Are they prepared to take on the following tasks: to maintain hope through the painful process of change; to recognize the divine presence in the signs of the times; to discern the right direction and appropriate time for action; and to empower one another as they move resolutely forward in the continuity of faith and tradition?

A Time of Transition

The recognition is growing that the world is in the midst of an unprecedented era of upheaval and transition. Here again the need for effective social analysis comes to the fore. Where does the church stand in the midst of all this upheaval? How deeply have ecclesial institutions been modified by the structures of society in the course of time? What distortions have emperors and monarchs caused in our ecclesial structures, our liturgy, our way of life? What positive and negative traits have been inherited from church association with different forms of government: aboriginal, imperial, monarchic, republican, democratic, or other?

Vatican II declared that the authentic church founded by Jesus Christ subsists in the Catholic Church. It retains its visible identity through history while remaining faithful to the initial founding gift. The church is hierarchical by nature. The laying on of hands empowers chosen leaders to oversee the communion of unity in diversity. Ordained ministerial leadership is meant to enhance, not replace, the responsibility for participation and decision-making, and the consequent rights, of all the baptized. The power of veto accorded certain officials can all too easily be abused. This power of veto's intended purpose is to safeguard authentic faith. It provides a reference when needed to the central and basic truth of the gospel as revealed by Jesus Christ and entrusted to the apostolic community. How closely do our church policies reflect the attitude of Jesus toward the people whom he met and the disciples he called to follow him? Is ministerial authority used for service or for self-enhancement? Did Christ advocate the use of power to suppress legitimate dissent?

The Liturgy as Key Source of Adult Religious Education

Jesus insisted that his disciples were not to lord it over others. He set the example of humble service and called on his followers to lay down their lives for one another. St. John's gospel associates the institution of the eucharist with the washing of the feet. How much of this tradition has withstood the test of time in our church structures?

The Christian community is called to sink its roots more deeply into the faith tradition, the scriptures, and the inspired teachings which constitute its heritage. From these sacred sources the believing community extracts the symbolic wealth which translates into creative energy through liturgy and transformative social action. Is the paschal mystery reflected in its assemblies of worship and in its ongoing corporate witness to the world?

It would be relatively easy to illustrate how the church has retained over the centuries some of the less desirable traits of society. Is the church prepared to recognize the complicity of some leaders in events that mark the darker hours of history? From the Roman

Empire the church acquired certain aspects of absolute imperial government. Some forms of liturgy have retained the trappings of royalty and the gestures of courtrooms. It is obvious that in these domains there is plenty of scope for self-examination and critique. What can the church learn from modern experience?

A Pastoral Church

The primary purpose of the church is to proclaim the Good News. This is achieved by calling people to personal and societal conversion. A commitment follows to transform the world through specific endeavours. Preference should be given to modest projects in which people with limited human resources can readily participate. Humanization that produces healing and resurrections is the touchstone. These successes illustrate how the reign of God has already been initiated in visible form while it awaits eschatological fulfillment. Proclaiming the mystery of hope to counter the prevailing culture of denial and dehumanization may be one of the most effective forms of modern preaching.

The church is not intended to build its own institutions or structures as if they were an end in themselves. It is meant to be totally at the service of the divine salvific purpose. Hence, its ministry is seen as one of solidarity and insertion in society, even more so than one of compassion and outreach toward the world from a safe distance. The faithful serve humankind most effectively by demonstrating how the gospel enhances human development even as it calls people to spiritual dedication.

There is a corollary here for adult faith development. This corollary calls for an essential focus on the ministry of service to society and to the whole of creation, particularly in the pursuit of justice. Being in communion with God has direct and vital social implications. Liturgy is directed dynamically toward mission even more than toward cultural insertion.

Rights and Duties

It is precisely this lay mission of praise and trans-formation in the midst of created reality which is the foundation of the laity's claims for full recognition in the church. Rights are inextricably linked with duties. They arise out of the dignity and responsibilities of baptized believers, created as they are in the image of God and called to be co-creators and partners in the divine plan of salvation.

Pope Paul VI once told a group of charismatic leaders that those who have rights also have the responsibility to claim them. Are church members encouraged to do that?

A Renewed Image of Church

Countless books have been written about contem-porary church renewal. It is amazing how pertinent this subject remains at the very time when numbers of people are inclined to write the church off as no longer signifi-cant. For indeed, what other institution is there that has been around for two thousand years and continues to claim the allegiance of millions of believers?

Therefore, it seems appropriate to reflect further on the church as contemporary structure. There is a continuous dialogical relationship between church and society. Where is the reign of God being proclaimed today? Messages of hope are found in modern movements of resistance and other new initiatives. Pope John XXIII signalled the promotion of women as a sign of the times. Other examples include the ecological movement, aborig-inal peoples' movements, and various expressions of the struggle for social justice, particularly with regard to the poor and less powerful.

Participants at the Second Vatican Council opted to focus their vision away from its predominantly European experience to a more global perspective. They de-empha-sized the vertical structural and sociological image uppermost in the minds of most church attendants and stressed the more biblical concept of the "people of God."

The entire membership of this people was envisaged as ministerial and missionary. Priority was assigned to the basic equality and responsibility of all the baptized before the hierarchical role of the ordained members was dealt with. This was indeed a major shift in the then contemporary thinking as well as a return to more traditional and more biblically inspired theology. All knowledge, theological as well as secular, is in constant evolution.

Inductive Methodology and Being Church

In the realm of theology, the previous unilateral emphasis on the deductive approach is being balanced by an inductive mode of discourse. Both the deductive and inductive methods are valid. To place them in opposition to one another is to partially cripple them. Both are essential for a comprehensive reflection on the saving purpose of God.

The church described as people of God creates the possibility to initiate, to participate, to accept responsibility for personal and communal faith development. When one depicts the church, or any other institution, primarily as structure, even in the broadest sense, one implies that there is an outside authority, a right way perceived as the exclusive way, the right answers as the only possible answers. This in turn suggests a pyramid of wisdom which can gradually be disseminated or imparted to the chosen few on special occasions. Wisdom, then, is not seen as the common heritage of everyone, equally accessible to all in the midst of normal daily occupations. We are still handicapped by this centuries-old, but not authentically traditional, dichotomy between a clerical caste of the initiated and the general membership. The "faithful" are considered primarily as recipients of knowledge imparted as it were from "above" by the "officials."

But when one considers the term "church" as being the entire people, a new dynamic emerges. The believing community is then constituted by the elements of life, of lived experience, where pain, struggle, hope and joy are evident. Healthy adult religious education is based on lived experience, reflection on scripture and tradition that honor that experience and challenge both individuals and groups to facilitate the rule of God.

The church is not an "either-or" phenomenon. There is present here a dynamic polarity which, by holding these opposites in tension, sets the stage for new life to develop. How exciting a prospect to consider what might happen! Might it be possible to coordinate the wisdom born of the presence of the Spirit of Jesus in the midst of all the pilgrim people with the wisdom acquired by the institutional church? Thus, the church, recognizing its purpose and mission, of serving others rather than being served, would again become renewed. Constantly examining its motives and assessing its service to the divine rule of love, would it not generate a genuine revolution, an explosion of joy and thanksgiving?

The Meaning of Hope

Some people tend to get discouraged when they consider the apparently insurmountable obstacles the church faces today. Judging by human standards, the condition of the world indeed may seem desperate. However, one does not need extensive contact with biblical sources or church history to appreciate that there have rarely been extensive periods of calm in the human pilgrimage on the stormy route to salvation. A reminder about what constitutes genuine hope may be helpful.

Authentic biblical hope is not generated in the calm and placid backwaters of history. It does not result from the linear projection of naive or optimistic forecasts, nor even from the tenacity of those who are prepared to make painful sacrifices to maintain security. The birth pangs of hope are felt when all else has failed. In that sense, it is conceived in despair. When concerted plans have been repeatedly frustrated, when the best of human inventiveness has proven futile, space is opened for a new kind of longing. Like the prophets of old, from the realization of their own inadequacy, believers turn to God and learn to rely on the Spirit of Christ. Then hope unfolds anew from the charred ruins of our worldly ambitions. Hope is the fruit of faith, of total trust in divine power. St. Paul learned to glory only in his confessed weakness, knowing that there the power and glory of God were made manifest.

Few periods in human history may prove more fitting than ours for the dawning of genuine hope. Significant initiatives suggest this is already happening. Small faith groups are mushrooming. One learns of a multitude of new beginnings occurring in local churches. A visit to a basic faith community, at home or even better in less developed countries, could provide an enriching experience. There, people gather to pray, to share, to celebrate, to plan, to mission one another, and to engage in a cause greater than themselves.

The Tradition of Synod Gathering and Faith Development

One speaks best of that which one has lived and experienced. It might be of interest therefore to mention the Peoples' Synod celebrated on Vancouver Island from 1986 to 1991. The diocese invited all believers to assemble in small groups and to share their experiences as members of their parish or local community. They were encouraged to compare their personal faith stories with the stories of their broader faith family, the church universal. These shared stories and comparisons provided the fertile soil for new ideas about the future of the church. A thousand suggestions were brought forward. These were collated, without any censuring whatever, and were made available to other people who wished to enrich them with their own experiences. Several hundred proposals ensued. They were later submitted to a process of communal faith discernment by ninety delegates chosen from across the diocese. Over four hundred proposals were approved, together with a renewed vision for the diocese. Priorities were agreed upon. A substantial diocesan agenda emerged spontaneously out of the storytelling, faith sharing, and communal spiritual discernment process. It reflected the workings of the Holy Spirit present in the midst of current events and the lived faith experience of the people. The new directions and vision were then officially promulgated. The proposals were offered as guidelines for all the parishes to implement. This is one illustration of how a particular church provided a contemporary structure for adult faith education and development.

This synod story is told in a book entitled *Forward in the Spirit—Challenge of the People's Synod*. Made available at the closing session, it was later widely distributed. The process was also outlined in a document known as *The Core Report*.[1] The texts serve as a basis for continued storytelling, prayer, reflection and invitation to conversion. As people continue to voice their hopes and concerns, a sense of family, of community, evolves in the presence of the Word made flesh. The voices heard in *Forward in the Spirit* encourage new stories, today's stories, today's solutions. Different issues may be generated. Reflection, prayer and participation in adult education groups may give birth to wisdom, may lead to implementation of the gospel and traditional values into society. Is this not a church as a contemporary structure for adult religious education?

From Vision to Action

For the church to struggle with and to embrace renewal is to be contemporary. People of God who commit themselves to the divine reign enter the realm of faith and hope. To gather men and women of vision, compassion, and ability is to develop community. For adults to deepen their faith by transforming society is to enter the prophetic. People who journey with God honor their being created in the image of God, rejoice in creation, and dance to the rhythm of the sacred.

DISCUSSION QUESTIONS

1. What do you mean when you use the word "church"?

2. What can church communities learn from the society to which they address the message of the gospel?

3. If you painted a mural representing the church, what features, shapes, and colors would you include?

4. What are the basic assumptions on which you build your pastoral efforts?

5. Are our parish rectories or offices centers of life, or rather administrative enclaves; do parish leaders go to the people, or are the people expected to make the first move?

6. How does your personal model of church work to promote continuous adult learning?

NOTES

1. *Forward in the Spirit: Challenge of the People's Synod and The Core Report* are obtainable from the Victoria Diocesan Centre, Victoria, British Columbia.

ABOUT THE AUTHOR

Bishop Remi J. De Roo was born in Swan Lake, Manitoba, on February 24, 1924. He obtained a Doctorate in Theology from the Angelicum University in Rome and has received five honorary degrees. He was appointed Bishop of Victoria October 31, 1962, and attended all four sessions of the Second Vatican Council (1962-1965). He has lectured widely and is well known for his advocacy of social justice and human rights.

3. QUESTIONS OF LIFE: QUESTIONS OF FAITH

Caryl Green

When describing their experience of church, many adults today speak of their pain and disillusionment: the church does not deal with us as adults! Rather, they experience the church as an authoritarian parent who interacts with them as children. Within the church adults find themselves receiving prescriptive guidelines on how to think and behave in matters that concern their faith. The church, as institution, does not encourage the questioning and discussion by which they seek to discover more about themselves, about the world, and about God. In this chapter I explore adult faith development and the church within the dynamic of a dialogue, a dialogue that honors both aspects of the questioning process, treating questions of faith and life as one. Within this framework, I explore freedoms for growth by presenting three cameos of faith development. These are accompanied by reflections on faith and development.

FREEDOMS FOR GROWTH

I have found that my own experience of parenting has influenced and shaped my reflections on adult faith development and the church. Parents try to provide a safe environment within which their children can learn about themselves and about their world. While children crave the security that such an environment offers, they also challenge the limits it creates. I have come to recognize that learning happens in the creative tension of, on one hand, living within the limits that have been established, and on the other, pushing beyond them to expand our

45

horizons—to discover the self within as well as the world beyond.

I realize that many adult educators will cringe to hear me speak of the church and adult faith development in terms of a secure learning environment and limits! Has not that very paternalistic approach contributed to the problems we experience in the church today? By comparing adult faith development and the church to the parent/child relationship I wish, however, to focus on the creative, life-giving tension that is inherent within that relationship. Both parent and child are intimately involved in the child's learning process and thus both are affected as the relationship evolves. Rather than establishing an either/or situation, I wish to speak of a both/and situation—both parents and child make up a family, just as both adult believers and the institutional church make up the believing community, the people of God. Although limits can be comforting, growth also requires certain freedoms.

The Freedom to Risk

In order to challenge the limits established by their parents, children must risk. Faced with parental authority, this risk can at times appear overwhelming. Yet risk they must. And the risk is possible because of the love and respect that are at the basis of a healthy parent/child relationship. (I say this while acknowledging the very real potential for hurt, neglect, and even abuse as it exists within the parent/child relationship and within the church community.)

As we seek to discover and to know the God of love more fully we must be prepared to take risks, to ask questions—of ourselves and of the church. Think of the many stories Jesus told of people who risked everything in order to touch and be touched by the God of love—the Samaritan woman, the woman with the hemorrhage, the man born blind, the children. These people challenged the limits or the definitions that their society (and their church) had placed on them—in order to eat, to drink, to hear, and to touch the new life offered them in Jesus. In risking everything they discovered the new life they sought.

But is the church a place where adults can risk? Can the church listen to what people are saying about God, especially if these stories challenge the established truth? Is the church a place where adults experience love and respect—whoever they are and whatever their life stories might be? The church has a responsibility to challenge us to grow beyond our blind spots and our points of denial. But the church's questioning must be based within a relationship of love, of respect, and of compassion. That questioning must be based within the dynamic of dialogue within which the questions arising from a person's own lived experience may be voiced, honored, and respected.

The Freedom to Question

In spite of their ambivalence regarding the church, many adults find themselves turning to the believing community when asking questions of faith. Why? Paul Tillich writes that "religion [as institution] is not the answer to the quest for unambiguous life, although the answer can only be received through religion."[1] What do we hope to hear from the church? Rooted in the words of scripture, the church speaks of a God of love, of life, and of human relationships. As adults we seek to understand the events of our daily lives using the insights we gain from these stories. Based in their lived experience, adult believers seek to enter into a dialogue with what the church teaches about God. That lived experience—with its brokenness, its hurt, and its despair—strains to hear the word of God, a word that gives hope and calls us to life. Walter Brueggemann states that "exoduses are happening all around us. Of a personal kind, in the pain and delight of growing up; of a social kind, in the upheavals and changes that make persons free and open up institutions;

of a visible, external kind and a hidden, internal kind. The Holy One, within and without, has not stopped freeing people and calling them to rejoice."[2]

But what of the life experiences that cannot be given voice within the church? Often adults choose not to speak of their experiences within the faith community for fear of being labelled and rejected. What of their exoduses, their freedom, and their rejoicing? Issues concerning human sexuality (for example, homosexual and lesbian love) and issues to do with the beginning and end of life (for example, birth control, abortion, and euthanasia) have been dealt with by the church primarily as issues of *morality*. The status given these moral teachings has been so great that adult believers often feel rejected by the church and, to some degree, rejected by God. In appearing to define *where* God can act and *whom* God can love, the church has acted as an obstacle to God's love, the very love that is needed to heal and transform people's lives. "Instead of transcending the finite in the direction of the infinite, institutional religion actually becomes a finite reality itself—a set of prescribed activities to be performed, a set of stated doctrines to be accepted, a social pressure group along with others, a political power with all the implications of power politics."[3]

What happens when the church, as institution, fails to listen to adults when they describe their experience of God *as they live it*? The dialogue falters. Growth in faith is compromised. People remain isolated in their hurt and in their searching. When adults lose the opportunity to give voice to their experience within the believing community, God's liberating word is also silenced. We are all empoverished as a result. Walter Vogels maintains:

> No life is without difficulties, but these can become an invitation to deepen our faithfulness. Laws cannot provide prefabricated answers to the complexities of life. We have to transcend the laws in freedom by the law of love. Love surpasses

everything. It can never be fixed in rules because it is always reaching further. Living according to the Bible does not lead to a static and passive life, but to a dynamic and active one of fresh commitments and new discoveries.[4]

What follows are three stories of faith development.[5] In order to assist the telling of each story I asked four questions: (a) Describe a situation or issue that provoked a questioning or reflection in your life; (b) Was religion/faith a factor in that questioning? (c) What role did the church play? and (d) What was the outcome? or How did you change as a result of this experience? I hope that I have honored the truth of these experiences—in the telling as well as in my discussion of the stories.

These stories reflect the immense joy as well as the deep pain that people experience in life. They reflect the obstacles people encounter in trying to find God—obstacles often created by the church. And they reflect the discovery that the church is not a thing but a *people*, the people of God. Faith is possible because of others who reveal God's love.

The stories speak of movement. Our lives have a beginning and have an end. They have direction. Often that direction is not clear. We are confused; we search; we lose our way. Darkness seems to engulf us. But we discover our way and our truth as much as we are able to know and experience God within our lives. This process of discovery involves our entire selves and lasts a lifetime. Carol Gilligan describes life as a "circling back to reappropriate in more profoundly human ways the connection and care from which we all begin."[6]

We discover God not only in times of crisis, but also in everyday events. These three stories speak of very different experiences—of being born with a disability and the questioning of that disability and of God; of friendships and how they reveal the God who lives in our midst; of a crisis in life and how the image of God was challenged during that time. These are stories of adults who have chosen to ask questions—of themselves, of others and of God—as they seek to grow in faith in light of their life experience.

THREE STORIES OF FAITH DEVELOPMENT

God's Love Revealed Through Disability

The following story describes a questioning that began at birth and that will certainly span a lifetime. How are life and love and God revealed in the very fabric of one's being—one's body?

Please describe a situation or an issue that provoked a questioning or reflection in your life. The issue that has provoked the most serious questioning in my life is the issue of my body. I have been disabled from birth; my disability is invisible. It has not been cured. I have been fortunate to meet many skilled professional people who, through the use of technology, have given me the hope of a *normal* life span. I have met many disabled people who have given me the hope that it is possible to live with a disability, and to live well. I have met many non-disabled people who do not see my disability and count me as one of them.

Was religion/your faith a factor in your questioning? For me, God has always been a part of the questioning of my body. The question of God's existence has never really been a question. God is the only one who could answer my questions. Can I live? How do I live? And does it matter whether or not I live?

What role did the church play? The church has played an important, pivotal role in the answers to the questions I have asked of God. It has done so in a very mysterious way—by asking me more questions which have broken through some errors and myths. What am I paying attention to? Why? Is this helpful? I must answer. I must pay attention not only with my eyes, my ears, my intellect, but with my whole body. I must attend to my body. I must attend to my body because my body is myself—and my self is not the enemy. My self is what lives, what lives through life, and yes, it does matter. My self is my friend. And this is grace. And grace does help.

What was the outcome? How did you change as a result of this experience? The outcome of this questioning has been to bring me to a body that is mine, a body that lives, a body that God created and loves. I have changed in this lifelong process of questioning. I can see my body as whole, complete when I can attend to my body with the whole of my body. I can live this way. The church helped to bring me to this place because it stopped and took the time to question me. Who is the church? The church has been those people who have stopped, questioned and listened.

God's Love Revealed Through Friendship

The following reflection demonstrates how, much like the experience of the disciples on the road to Emmaus, God is found in the sharing of our stories.

Please describe a situation or an issue that provoked a questioning or reflection in your life. Friendships have challenged me profoundly: as my friends have shared with me their life journeys and I've shared my own, I've come to recognize the enormous complexity of being human. I've come to know very intimately some of these stories, and my own. These people's very *lovability* is rooted in the twists and turns of their lives, in the very parts they would edit out.

Was religion/your faith a factor in your questioning? There's a kind of irony in the fact that so much of our life-giving energy comes from situations that many religious people would judge harshly. Oftentimes the expectation of such a judgment was one of the obstacles that people had to overcome even to voice their story. These experiences forced us all to go beyond our knee-jerk images of God to find a God who was a God of compassion, a God whose sole concern was not with issues of sexuality, for instance, but with integrity and faithfulness. Having to acknowledge the complexity and ambiguity of things both in my own life and in the lives of others caused my whole perspective to shift. And consequently, I have had to rediscover who God might be.

What role did the church play? Formally, none. However, most of us were/are very involved in our faith tradition. It was always a backdrop against which, or a context within which, our dialogue took place. In a sense, it was a dialogue between siblings trying to discover how to remain in our common home. Building these relationships was my first teacher on the way of compassion. The journey enabled me to discover that I was home in a profound way. I've been challenged, reassured, and consoled that I do belong, not just with those whose stories I know, but in the wider church.

What was the outcome? How did you change as a result of this experience? It brought me nose-to-nose with the fundamental reality of Christian existence: salvation is not earned. It could not possibly be. It is truly a gift born of God's graciousness. Our lives are such a tapestry of grace and sin, giftedness and brokenness that even our most Herculean efforts could not save us. Face-to-face with that reality, I recognized only three options: abandon faith altogether; commit myself to the unending task of trying to earn salvation; or accept the gift. The second seemed impossible; the first led only to despair; the third, though still difficult, seems best to honor both God and humanity. If I dare let God be God, then perhaps all of us can dare to be ourselves—broken and blessed. Dare I that much love? Some days it's easier than others. Then I remember me and us, and the story of the Christ, and I know there's no other way.

I have come to know that I am not alone. I really can live my life out of this profound conviction—even when I feel most abandoned. I am never utterly abandoned. Over and over again, the compassion and open hearts of my friends have taught me this. Life is good. It is worthy of trust. Sometimes I forget that. Sometimes I don't believe it. But then there's always someone, something, to remind me.

God's Love Revealed Through Crisis

The following story offers a glimpse into the faith journey of a woman who grappled with the decision of having an abortion.

Please describe a situation or an issue that provoked a questioning or reflection in your life. When I was in my twenties, I had an abortion. I knew that my church was against abortion and I knew that my family was as well. But somehow, in a time of great confusion and conflict, I made the decision to have an abortion. My decision was made in great distress. However, I do remember that I felt that this was the decision I needed to make. God was with me—somehow—though my head told me otherwise. After all, my church is quick to condemn abortion and certainly any woman who has one. I remember feeling alone, lost. The weight of my church's position made it difficult to find my way. Yet I made the decision and had the abortion. With years of soul searching and reflection, understanding has emerged.

Was religion/your faith a factor in your questioning? Definitely yes. My action challenged so many—everything—of my beliefs. I held an image of God as father, as judge, as far-off and distant (on his chair). I fought against this image in coming to my decision and for years afterward. Could this God love me in spite of what I was about to do or had done?

As well, my image/understanding of church—was the church, as an institution, going to define my image of myself as sinner, unworthy of God's love? Could I receive God's love only after asking for forgiveness? From whom? Or could the church be with me, believing in the power of God's love to make new?

What role did the church play? I found I needed to leave the church for a time. The words, on Sundays especially, were laden with values and, in my searching, my vulnerability, I found it too hard to sit there. I cried a lot. Individuals within the church supported me, listening to my story, to my searching, to my pain. In their love and acceptance I found healing and in their belief in a God of infinite love, I found new life.

What was the outcome? How did you change as a result of this experience? My image of God changed drastically. I came to know and experience the God of love and of faithfulness. From an experience of death I discovered new life. God's love brought healing to many past hurts and opened new beginnings. I came to understand the ambiguity of life—to know the pain most of us walk around with in one form or another. I am less quick to judge. I realize that within each person's story there is hurt, confusion, despair as well as love, trust and hope. God lives within that complexity. I define myself less through the church as institution but see the church as people. I feel such compassion for people in pain, in times of deep brokenness. I know God's transforming love.

REFLECTIONS ON FAITH AND DEVELOPMENT

These three stories reflect what it is to grow in faith—to risk, to search, to question, and to discover. Growth in faith involves pain, confusion, joy, new life, and new faith. This is life, a life in God. Faith can often appear to be a set of beliefs to which a believer must give his/her assent. Put rather simplistically, the church has set out certain *rules* to help the believer find the proper way to live, to live a life pleasing to God, to live righteously. These rules, created by the church's teaching office, are to be accepted as presented. If transgressed, forgiveness must be sought.

This above notion of faith or of religion does not encourage the dialogue between life experience and church teachings that is necessary for faith development. For one thing, the assent required is only of the head and does not invite total involvement: body and soul. Carol Ochs describes how, at times, we find ourselves "faced with making a rational choice in a domain where every fiber of our being tells us that the choice has nothing at all to do with reason. In grappling with such a choice, we become aware of the structures that hold rationality together. This awareness forces us beyond rationality into a state of radical aloneness with unshared categories for thinking about reality."[7] God is found even where our head tells us *No!* God is discovered in the stillness of our hearts, when the head allows the heart to speak. Winston Gooden writes that "knowing that one's life is purposeful and good is not only a matter of reasoning; it is beyond reason, accepted without logical proof yet maintained by commitment and action. To reason out the integrity of a life would perhaps lead to madness. The act of maintaining a sense of meaning is a passionate act that involves the gut as much as the head."[8] It may be a lot easier to accept what others say—and a lot safer—but we discover God in risking to be wrong. We find God when we find we are loved even when we think we are most unlovable.

Faith as Process

Much has been written about the *stages* of faith development. The movement underlying these theories seems to create the expectation that there is an ideal to be reached. Carol Ochs questions the journey metaphor prevalent in traditional Western spirituality because "inherent in the metaphor is the notion of a goal."[9] While I agree with a sense of movement in faith development, I perceive that movement as a spiral that gathers our experiences together as we grow through life. Within this spiral there are moments of intense questioning, even crises, as well as moments of integration wherein we live out the new truths we discover in the questioning. Gabriel Moran speaks of conversion as "a circling back on oneself and a recapitulating of life at a deeper level."[10] He questions the image of *ladder* that is inherent in the stage theories because of its statement on the way God is revealed. "A ladder downward all too easily shifts into being a ladder upward. And once the moral life has been reduced to invariant, sequential, hierarchical steps up a ladder, then proclamations of divine descent simply conflict with the established way of moral thinking."[11]

Winston Gooden also challenges this sequential, hierarchical theory of development. Gooden sees faith development (faith-work) as a process,

> the continuous integrative shaping of one's life in accordance with the overarching framework of meaning one has chosen. This shaping and integrating become most crucial when the person confronts critical existential issues. Situations such as failure, loss, the need for important choices often threaten to disrupt the organization and meaning of life. The work of integrating these experiences into the self and broadening one's framework of understanding is faith-work.[12]

Faith develops when we find ourselves face-to-face with questions of life—of birth and of death—of suffering and of brokenness. We find ourselves caught up in an experience that seeks an answer. Our lives are continually in a process of transformation whereby our questions find their answers in the living out of the questions—in dialogue with self, others and with God. Walter Vogels writes that:

> To live according to the Bible requires openness to God. This is a summons to be honest with ourselves, to live in truth, to live authentically. The answers to the many questions which sooner or later appear in life, and the ideals that we pursue, cannot be found in books. We have to search out how we must live if we are to be at peace with ourselves and, thus, with God. Each of us has to listen to other people, to the world, and, above all, to our conscience. When we attain clear

insight we must then find the courage to accept it
and to live by it.[13]

Within any theory of faith development there must be
room for intergenerational dialogue. Adult educators
often support the theory of intergenerational learning,
but offer little in the way of concrete examples or suggestions. In the gospel, Jesus says, "Let the little children
come, and do not stop them; for it is to such as these that
the kingdom of God belongs. I tell you solemnly, anyone
who does not welcome the kingdom of God like a little
child will never enter it" (Luke 18: 15-17). Children have a
lot to teach us about love, about life and death, about God,
and about faith. Children reveal truths that adults often
hide from or cover up. Carol Ochs writes that we "pay lip
service to the significance of the experience of little
children, but in fact their perceptions, their dependencies,
their pre-linguistic being are rarely explored in theological
systems."[14]

We learn from children of all ages as well as adults of
all ages. Gabriel Moran suggests that "a theory of moral
development has to include an old person sitting quietly
with a child."[15] Both children and older adults often find
themselves without a voice. What love, what wealth of
experience we are missing! In silencing these voices the
faith development of adults is empoverished.

A definition of faith development, taken from the
children's book, *The Velveteen Rabbit* might read as follows:

"What is REAL?" asked the Rabbit one day...
"Real isn't how you are made," said the Skin Horse.
"It's a thing that happens to you. When a child loves you
for a long, long time, not just to play with, but REALLY
loves you, then you become Real."
"Does it hurt?" asked the Rabbit.
"Sometimes," said the Skin Horse... "When you are
Real you don't mind being hurt."
"Does it happen all at once, like being wound up," he
asked, "or bit by bit?"

"It doesn't happen all at once," said the Skin Horse. "You become. It takes a long time. That's why it doesn't often happen to people who break easily, or have sharp edges, or who have to be carefully kept. Generally, by the time you are Real, most of your hair has been loved off, and your eyes drop out and you get loose in the joints and very shabby. But these things don't matter at all, because once you are Real you can't be ugly, except to people who don't understand."[16]

EXPERIENCE REVEALING FAITH

In Genesis we read how when God spoke, the world in its many forms was created; and God saw that it was good. Human beings are created in God's image, and we are good. God exists in the very depth of our being and it is there—at a truly gut-level—that we know we are loved by God.

In and Through Disability

All that God creates reveals God's love in the world. Jesus, as Word of God, reveals that love most clearly. God's word is spoken in and through each and every one of us. Being born with a disability begs the question—did God intend this? Did God give me this body for a reason? Just what can this disability reveal of a God who loves? Or perhaps the questions should be turned around: What does God say about this body, this disability and this person—"in whom I take great pleasure"?

We are able to love inasmuch as we allow God's love to work in our lives. Paul Tillich describes how, while we experience God within us, at the same time we know that experience is incomplete: we are grounded in the divine but the deepest movement of our spirit is "toward the recovery of our essential participation in the Godhead."[17] Based in our life experience, we discover the God that is within, yet we also experience the absence of God. We discover the great capacity we have for love, but also the capacity to hurt. We discover we are able to give life, but also to take life. God knows all this. So we live in this creative tension—believing that God both dwells within *and* draws us to greater fullness of life.

Questions arise from our lived experience—whether from within, from the feelings we have about ourselves, or from external events in our lives. Winston Gooden describes how "when the established patterns are challenged either by failure or by success, the individual must construe the contents of experience in new, more universal ways in order to integrate the threatening experience and maintain a life of wholeness and integrity."[18] For the woman born with a disability, the threat to her sense of *wholeness and integrity* arose from the very experience of her body. In her questioning and in her responding to the church's questions, she discovered the truth that her strength lies in her disability—because her disability does not define her. Her life, and that includes her body, speaks of God's love for those who are willing to listen.

In and Through Friendships

Friendships, like faith, develop over time. Within a friendship there are moments of intense sharing combined with the *living-out* of that intimacy, the making real. Friendships often unfold in mysterious ways. When face-to-face with the mystery of love, our response can only be acceptance. This is a pure gift. Carol Ochs explains that "the love that we receive is the same as the love that we give. The gift of being loved is also the gift of being free to love."[19]

For many, friendships are a haven where the ambiguities of life may be shared. In the very security of a friendship we discover our vulnerability. Carol Ochs writes that relationship is "a time of wonder—discovering who we are in the presence of the other and discovering who the other person is. It is also a time of fear—longing to be known but feeling we are vulnerable."[20] Friendships have a way of inviting life's hurts to be spoken and, in that speaking, new beginnings are made possible. In the compassionate love of a friend, we touch the compassionate love of our God. And in that touch we are changed.

So often we find we are drawn to people who are different from ourselves. Within a friendship those differences must be respected in order to reach beyond them, in order to know the other in their truth. Because of a friend's own unique experience and perspective on life, we often receive from him or her an image or a reflection of ourselves that is unexpected. With this comes new insight into our experience; we are opened to new possibilities, to unexpected ways of finding meaning in our experience. Walter Brueggemann, in describing the element of *mystery* in our lives, points to the "remarkable experience we have that the factors and persons in our lives whom we know best and trust most are precisely the ones who continue to surprise and heal us and call us to newness."[21]

In and Through an Abortion

Winston Gooden mentions that "where one's self-concept and identity no longer are viable in the light of what happens so one must find a new way of envisioning one's life both past and present that will bring meaning out of the chaos of one's present experience;...a new image must emerge."[22] In the crisis of identity and meaning brought about by the abortion, this woman's image of God was replaced by a new image. Within the darkness and confusion, a God of compassion and of love emerged who gave meaning to her life, both past and future. "Faith seems to grow out of the dark nights of the soul in its confrontations at the limits of life. It is often easier and more comfortable not to confront nonbeing than to confront it and lose in the process."[23] Faced with an abortion, this woman risked losing everything—the love and acceptance of God and that of her family as well. Would God and her family still be there? In fact, she discovered what Walter Brueggemann describes when he states:

Such events, exodus or resurrection, are glimpses of the Holy One. We know him as he turns our life toward wholeness. Such a notion of the Holy One is a distinctive, if not peculiar notion of who God is. It means that we do not perceive God as a rule-giver, as an establisher of right and wrong, or as guarantor of the status-quo. Rather, God acts in the moment of the turn. And the rest of our faith consists of reflection upon those moments in which our lives are changed. Such moments address us and insist that we be transformed. Such events claim us. They overwhelm us with a demand, which then comes to be morality.[24]

All three women referred to the pivotal role that *people* have played in their faith journeys. In her research on moral development, Carol Gilligan found that women tend to define themselves through their relationships with others. When faced with conflicting demands or expectations, a woman tries to solve the problem in such a way that no one is hurt. Whereas Kohlberg identified a morality of *rights*, Gilligan's research uncovered a morality of *care* and of *responsibility*. "The essence of a moral decision is the exercise of choice and the willingness to accept responsibility for that choice."[25] In the church, the issue of human sexuality has largely been treated with a morality of rights rather than a morality of responsibility and care. Faced with an abortion or any other moral issue, the dilemma becomes: How does one live *responsibly* and *lovingly* within a church that speaks only of *rights*?

To Love as We Are Loved

Faith is not meant to remain at a personal level. There must always be an aspect of faith that reaches out to others, that is communal. We are known, recognized as being children of God, through our lives of faith. We are called to witness to God's love—to bring greater peace in our relationships and to bring justice to our world. We cannot witness to that which we have not experienced first hand—God's love, peace and justice acting in our own lives.

We discover God's love in the fragility of life. God's love gives meaning to the suffering and death that we experience in so many ways in our lives. God's love touches and transforms our lives so we can love more deeply. The disciple John writes, "If you make my word your home, you will indeed be my disciples, you will learn the truth, and the truth will make you free" (John 8: 31). How can we love if we do not first know ourselves to be loved? Is there any experience that God has not experienced first? That God refuses to be associated with? God loves us into wholeness so we may live more fully, in the image of our Creator. Growing in faith implies living that creative tension of knowing and not knowing the God of love, of experiencing the *now* and the *not yet* of the kingdom. T. S. Eliot evokes that wondrous relationship of faith that beckons us ever deeper into ourselves and into God:

> With the drawing of this Love and the voice of this
>   Calling
> We shall not cease from exploration
> And the end of all our exploring
> Will be to arrive where we started
> And know the place for the first time.
> Through the unknown, remembered gate
> When the last of earth left to discover
> Is that which was the beginning;
> At the source of the longest river
> The voice of the hidden waterfall
> And the children in the apple-tree
> Not known, because not looked for
> But heard, half-heard, in the stillness
> Between two waves of the sea.
> Quick now, here, now, always—
> A condition of complete simplicity
> (Costing not less than everything)

And all shall be well and
All manner of things shall be well
When the tongues of flame are in-folded
Into the crowned knot of fire
And the fire and the rose are one.[26]

DISCUSSION QUESTIONS

1. Reflect on your own faith development using the four reflection questions in this chapter.

2. In your community what opportunities exist to gather together and share your life experiences?

3. How does your community encourage dialogue at its various levels of organization?

4. What opportunities exist to affirm children and older adults and to encourage their contribution in your community?

5. How does your Sunday worship speak to people's experience? How does your Sunday worship reflect the truth of the God of love?

6. How are people made to feel welcome in your community—both newcomers and those who have belonged for years?

NOTES

1. Paul Tillich, *Systematic Theology* (Chicago: The University of Chicago Press, 1963), Vol. 3, p. 106. In this book, Tillich addresses the problem of ambiguity (and our search for the *unambiguous* life) through an examination of the symbols of faith and of our modern day culture.

2. Walter Brueggemann, *Living Toward a Vision: Biblical Reflections on Shalom* (Philadelphia: United Church Press, 1982), p. 65. This book is a collection of essays on the biblical vision of peace and justice. Brueggemann's use of the images of exodus and resurrection

breaks open these theological truths in a way that
stirs the imagination and offers hope.

3. Paul Tillich, *Systematic Theology*, Vol. 3, p. 99.

4. Walter Vogels, *Becoming Fully Human: A Biblical Perspective* (Ottawa, Ont.: Novalis, 1988), p. 53. This book
illustrates how the Bible offers insights into our
relationships with others, with God, and with the
world. The Bible does not provide answers to the
specific questions we may have; rather, we must start
with a reflection on our own experience in light of
biblical truths.

5. Although all three stories were submitted by women,
the insights offered by their experiences have to do
with insights into the experience of being *human.* I
would like to thank the women who agreed to share
their stories—for the risk they have taken in giving
voice to their personal experience. I thank them for
their courage and for the profound gift that their
stories represent.

6. Carol Gilligan, *In a Different Voice: Psychological Theory
and Women's Development* (Cambridge, Mass.: Harvard
University Press, 1982), p. 90. This book looks at the
question of moral development from the perspective
of women's experiences. Gilligan hopes to develop a
new theory of development that takes into account
the lives of *both* women and men.

7. Carol Ochs, *Women and Spirituality.* (Totowa, N.J.:
Rowman & Allanheld, 1983), p. 39. Ochs offers insights
drawn from the experience of mothers and other
women to create an expanded notion of spirituality
that takes into account the earthy, relational experiences of life and of God.

8. Winston Gooden, "Responses and Comments from
an Adult Development Perspective," in *Faith
Development in the Adult Life Cycle*, ed. Kenneth Stokes
(New York: W.H. Sadlier, 1982), p. 97. Starting from
the understanding that faith is not a moral issue,

Gooden explores faith development (*faith-work*) as a question of maintaining a sense of meaning and integrity in one's life.

9. Ochs, *Women and Spirituality*, p. 138.

10. Gabriel Moran, *No Ladder to the Sky: Education and Morality* (San Francisco: Harper & Row, 1987), p. 5.

11. Ibid., p. 7.

12. Gooden, "Responses and Comments," p. 101.

13. Vogels, *Becoming Fully Human*, p. 53.

14. Ochs, *Women and Spirituality*, p. 25.

15. Moran, *No Ladder to the Sky*, p. 172. Moran, considering the lived, religious experience of adults, rejects the theories of development that are based on a hierarchical image. We need to explore and be open to different contributions and different images that integrate our experience and that don't transcend it.

16. Margery Williams, *The Velveteen Rabbit* (New York: Simon & Schuster, n.d.).

17. John Dourley, C. G. Jung and Paul Tillich, *The Psyche as Sacrament* (Toronto: The Inner City Books, 1981), p. 30. Dourley combines the theories of Jung and Tillich in an examination of the how religion/faith is intrinsic to the human soul. The manner in which we deal with this force will either bring growth or cause fragmentation. Both Jung and Tillich base their theories in the experience we have of the divine within.

18. Gooden, "Responses and Comments," p. 104.

19. Ochs, *Women and Spirituality*, p. 92.

20. Ibid., p. 115.

21. Brueggemann, *Living Toward a Vision*, p. 170.

22. Gooden, "Responses and Comments," p. 105.

23. Ibid., p. 99.

24. Brueggemann, *Living Toward a Vision*, p. 66.

25. Gilligan, *In a Different Voice*, p. 67. The issue of moral dilemma and moral decision-making is brought to light in the case study of women facing the possibility of an abortion.

27. T. S. Eliot, *Four Quartets*. (London: Faber and Faber, 1944), p. 48.

ABOUT THE AUTHOR

Caryl Green is presently working in the area of program planning and implementation for the Faculty of Theology, Saint Paul University, Ottawa. Since 1987 she has been involved in the development and implementation of the Summer Institute of Pastoral Liturgy, Saint Paul University. Caryl has worked as a writer and editorial assistant for the Adult Portfolio, National Office of Religious Education (Canadian Conference of Catholic Bishops), the Archdiocese of Ottawa, Novalis publishers, and various other associations. She holds a degree in biology from Queen's University, Kingston and a degree in theology from Saint Paul University, Ottawa. Caryl is married and has three children.

4. ADULT LEARNING
IN A RELIGIOUS CONTEXT

Margaret Fisher Brillinger

A sense of call is integral to the Christian life. Whether the call is a dramatic confrontation, such as Isaiah's or Paul's, or whether it is a quiet unfolding over time, people's response is an ongoing daily walk that takes travellers into ever-expanding awareness. Being called and responding provide a vision, a sense of direction to guide people's lives, a well of hope and purposefulness.

Churches are in a unique position to offer opportunities for people to refine or renew their vision of their lives, their faith community, and the world. They minister to people at all phases of the life cycle. Many seek the guidance and support of the church at critical turning points in their lives, such as marriage, birth and death. Through study groups, liturgy, committees, and outreach programs, the church has opportunities to facilitate intentionally people's faith learning and development throughout the life span.

In this chapter we as educators will expand our view of faith development from something that is done to the learner in a classroom setting to a daily ongoing journey of discovery and meaning-making. We will see that faith is not something that is taught or even learned; it is a dynamic unfolding of meaning which informs our ways of working and loving and living in the world. Then we shall explore adult educational principles that provide frameworks for planning religious education programs. Finally, we will reflect on the implications of these concepts for adult religious educators.

THE LEARNING CRUCIBLE

Learning is an exciting and dynamic process that involves the whole person in a journey of discovery. For Christians, learning is a crucible for refining their vocation in the world. In this section we expand our understanding of learning to appreciate more fully its conversion and empowering potential.

Learning as Creation

Learning is creating. For those who believe in a Creator God, creation is a sacred act. In the process of creating, people are engaged in the making of something brand-new. A learning episode is a container of time and space that holds energy for enlightenment and empowerment. It is a sacred moment when the energy of that space is being redirected and transformed into new perspectives and understandings. Both teacher and student share responsibility for the movement of this energy. Crucial to the process is the development of trust that whatever emerges in this space is relevant, no matter how absurd it may seem at first glance.

In *Teaching and Religious Imagination*, Maria Harris describes the work of teachers as "creating new possibilities on every teaching occasion, as continually offering to others the opportunity to take the material presented and to reform and recreate it in and through themselves." She continues by stating that "as long as creation is at the center of teaching, what seem like final solutions are merely tentative—the status quo can always be changed."[1]

The activity of creating is a process of giving flesh or meaning to the subject matter. As learners make sense of their daily experiences, their unfolding faith is constantly pointing to new possibilities for expression in their relations and work. Harris talks about the "incarnation, embodiment, giving-form-to, giving-flesh-to subject matter."[2]

Both educator and learner interact as co-creators. Both are students and both are teachers, engaged in a process of co-creating, of making new meaning from the experiences and information at hand. In coming to fresh understandings, they discover implications for carrying out their beliefs in their daily interactions in the world. Concepts and ideas, knowledge and belief are patiently transformed into new behaviors and attitudes in everyday lives.

The act of creating, by its very nature, is messy. There may be false starts, risk-taking, detours, failures. These are all part of the creative process. Even so-called "mistakes" belong. When people examine their "mistakes" or doubts or failures in order to discover what messages they need to hear from them, every experience has the potential for new learnings. All participants and all experiences in the educational situation, by their very presence, are embodying what it means to be human, what it means to be growing and learning as children of God. Whether the learning experience occurs within a religious context or not, the sacred act of creating new meanings is at work. All significant learning becomes part of the energy of the Creator; all experience has been God-given and has the potential for learning.

Holistic Learning

Traditionally in Western thought, we divide people, things, and ideas into little pieces so that we are no longer aware of the connections between them. We think in terms of "us" or "them," "male" or "female," "material" or "spiritual," "sacred" or "secular." This dualistic perspective has led to fragmentation and isolation.

In *Care of the Soul*, Thomas Moore[3] expresses his belief that psychology and spirituality need to be seen as one. He suggests that the way out of dualistic attitudes is to foster care of the soul in our ordinary everyday lives. Indigenous peoples have long believed in the interconnectedness of all life. Their teachings point to our relatedness as living creatures to the earth and to one another.[4]

The challenge for education within a religious context is to uphold a vision of the wholeness and the holiness of all life and learning. Holistic education emphasizes the importance of integrating the multiple facets of human learners in order to help them appreciate their connections with other people, the earth, and a higher being. In becoming attuned to these relationships, people appreciate the unity and interconnectedness of all life.

Significant learning involves the whole person—mind, emotions, body, spirit. John Miller describes the focus of holistic education as being "the relationship between linear thinking and intuition, the relationship between mind and body, the relationships among various domains of knowledge, the relationship between the individual and community, and the relationship between self and Self. In the holistic curriculum the student examines these relationships so that he/she gains both an awareness of them and the skills necessary to transform the relationships where it is appropriate."[5]

A holistic education approach enables people to engage fully and actively in the process of learning. It transforms the fragmenting, dualistic perspective into a synthesis which celebrates wholeness and which affirms the interconnectedness of knowledge and all life.

Religious Learning Throughout Life

As children, much of our early religious and identity formation is largely at an emotional level, learned within the context of family and social networks. Knowledge is passed on from external authority figures to children in a transmission model of education. As individuals move into adolescence and adulthood, the application of reason to the emotional underpinnings becomes critical. The task for adults is to involve themselves reasonably and intelligently as well as emotionally in their ongoing faith journey so that their expanding understandings provide guidelines for daily behavior. This is a transformational model of education which involves the whole person in the process of learning. Being called to our full personhood as children of God necessitates this ongoing learning.

Bill Marrevee compares this repeated faith-appropriation to the marriage relationship in which "the original yes-word needs to be reaffirmed...in the light of new circumstances." This does not invalidate the original vow of commitment but recognizes that "at the moment of the original yes-word, its full scope cannot be foreseen. New facets of it...will inevitably surface with new experiences that mark our history."[6]

People *are* learning throughout their lives. With the increasing complexity of our world, lifelong learning and adapting are absolutely necessary even for basic survival, let alone for tasting the fullness of life. Developmental needs require that we constantly reexamine old frameworks for viewing the world as we outgrow earlier perceptions. As we broaden our views to become increasingly aware of the rich complexity and interconnections of our world, we must engage in ongoing learning in order to continue to develop thoughtful guidelines for behavior. More than simply adding pieces of knowledge to people's stockpile, adult religious educators are in a position to help people expand their understanding of their vocation to live responsibly on this planet. The ethical and moral issues confronting all require responses from people with a vision and a sense of mission as they develop a maturing faith over their lifespan.

Learning as Transformation

A transmission model of education moves facts and information from one person to another. With this approach, a teacher or expert in the content area imparts knowledge to the learners. The degree of participant involvement can vary greatly. In some instances, the focus may be quite superficial and removed from learners' personal lives.

However, a transformational model of education invites participants to be deeply involved in exploring issues and interacting with the subject matter and with one another. The learners' fundamental sense of themselves is being shifted and shaken as their perspective is transformed. Religious conversion is an example of a profound transformation whereby individuals come to see themselves, others, their ministry, and their relationship with God in a fresh way. A living faith has to be reexamined and reappropriated over and over as new life experiences point the way to more mature meanings and beliefs. People continue to learn about God's plan for their lives on a daily basis. Conversion, then, is an ongoing journey of discovery and expanding awareness rather than a once-in-a-lifetime, static event.

The transformation goes beyond a private, internal reframing. As people expand their understanding of their purpose in life, they move out to see their mission in the world. They involve themselves in work and relationships to help transform communities and the world. Whether they choose to work to bring about change in less developed countries or with aboriginal communities, with victims of political oppression or victims of family violence, with ignorance or illness, with social injustices or economic poverty, their maturing faith finds active expression in a calling to use their energies to empower whole communities and societies. In turn, the very act of struggling to right wrongs and minister to pain in the larger world creates yet more opportunities for deepening their own faith understanding.

Adult religious educators help people explore life-altering issues as they examine profound questions of faith. A transformational model of education that engages participants in deeply personal involvement and dialogue is thus essential for meaningful learning about one's faith. There are a number of adult education principles that have been empirically derived for promoting such a transformational model of education.

ADULT EDUCATION PRINCIPLES

In this section we turn to the field of adult education to provide principles that will guide religious educators as they incorporate this broadened vision of learning in their practice. These principles have been derived from successful elements of practice.

Principles of Adult Education
Relevant to Religious Education

Think of a really good learning experience you have had where you were growing in your understanding of your faith. Suspend all critical judgment for a moment as you let yourself slip back to that experience. Recall who was there and what was going on. Allow the feelings of the occasion to wash over you again. In your mind's eye, trace back over the happenings of that positive learning episode.

Now begin to focus on aspects of the experience that contributed to its value. What factors made this so beneficial to your faith journey? What ingredients helped make it such a positive moment for you? What was going on that contributed to your spiritual growth?

Then think of a negative learning experience you have had. Take yourself back to the events and people and feelings of that time. As you let yourself relive it, begin to identify some of the factors that contributed to its negative impact. What elements got in the way of your spiritual learning?

During a positive learning experience, people often report factors such as trusting the teacher or group leader, the teacher's respect for the learners, a comfortable atmosphere, safety for sharing and expressing doubts, and group interaction and discussion. During a negative learning episode, people often report factors such as low level of trust, little input from students, authoritative teacher viewed as expert, low group interaction, conflicting goals and expectations, little listening, and a tense atmosphere.

These positive and negative learning experiences indicate some important principles and assumptions about how adults learn. Many authors such as Brookfield,[7]

Brundage and MacKeracher,[8] Kidd,[9] Knowles,[10] and Smith[11] have described various factors underlying adult education which call forth and nurture rich growth for adults. Here I condense some of these factors into five points that are generally acknowledged as basic principles.

1. Learning is a process occurring within the learners and controlled primarily by them. Carl Rogers[12] believed that anything that can be taught to another is relatively unimportant and that knowledge which springs from people's own inner system of making meaning cannot be communicated or transmitted directly to another. Consequently, the educator's appropriate role is more of a coach, supporter, challenger, and facilitator and less of a teller, imparter of knowledge, advisor, or expert.

2. People learn best in an environment that encourages self-esteem and interdependence. Adults need to be treated with respect. They bring with them a rich background of life experience which informs and is informed by the content of the current learning experience. They have much to offer one another in a collaborative, dialogical climate of sharing.

3. Adults prefer to participate in the planning and decision-making related to the learning. Stephen Brookfield states that "adults learn best when they feel the need to learn and when they have a sense of responsibility for what, why, and how they learn."[13] They want to clarify their learning needs and provide input into the structure of the event, including participating in the evaluation of their own learning outcomes.

4. Adults expect relevance and timeliness for their learning. There is a moment of readiness when their journey takes them to a point of openness and receptivity for the learning event. They want the learning to be pertinent to their life journey, with immediately useful application. Brundage and MacKeracher refer to people's feelings and needs as being "present-tense...directly related to the learner's current life experience, tasks, relationships and problems and indirectly related to his

past experience. These present-tense feelings and needs must be respected and recognized."[14]

5. People have different preferred ways of taking in and processing information, and of responding to learning situations. Smith suggests that "adults differ as to how they go about thinking and solving problems as well as in their preferences for methods, environments, and structure." As they interact with peers, they struggle in their own ways with issues and tasks current to their lives and work. Learning is enhanced by various activities and structures that appeal to a range of learning styles. Smith goes even further when he says that the knowledge of learning style is useful not only to be an effective adult educator but also "in becoming an effective adult learner."[15]

In order to increase knowledge of adult learning concepts, I encouraged educators to pay attention to what is going on inside learners.[16] Adult religious educators who are aware of the principles and conditions for effective learning usually design programs that are faithful to these principles and that are sensitive to the needs and backgrounds of the learners.

Learning Grounded in Our Own Faith Journey

Significant faith learning is grounded in our own experience. It does not come from outside ourselves. As we experience and then reflect on the experience in order to make sense of it, we develop insights which inform our future actions. The cyclical process of experiencing, reflecting, making meaning, and applying leads to a new experience, which we in turn take note of, conceptualize, and from which increased understanding is guided in subsequent behaviors. As the cycle continues throughout our lives, we engage in a lifelong process of learning from our experiences.

David Kolb[17] has given us a model to grasp the cyclical nature of the learning process against the backdrop of varied learning styles. His model illustrates two dimensions of cognitive growth and learning: preferred way of perceiving (taking in), and preferred way of processing (fitting in).

The *perceiving* dimension is on a concrete-abstract continuum, whereas the *processing* dimension is on a reflective-active continuum. On the first dimension, learners range from those who like to become involved with tangible, personal activities, to those who prefer a more detached, analytical approach. On the second dimension, learners range from those who contemplate application by reflective, internalized thoughts to those who jump in to try out possibilities through action. Kolb avoids evaluative judgments of these four kinds of learners, demonstrating how each style has its strengths and weaknesses.

In a group, there are likely to be all four kinds of learners. The variety can contribute to the energy of movement through the cycle. As learners connect with their own stories and experiences (*concrete experience*), they can be encouraged to reflect on them (*reflective observation*) in order to organize experience into meaningful frameworks (*abstract conceptualization*) for guiding future behavior (*active experimentation*).

An owned faith is grounded in the stories of the learners. When we open ourselves to observing and making sense of our life experience, we grow and develop as children of God. This is the journey of growing into the fullness of the likeness of Christ.

The cyclical nature of learning engages us in a dynamic, lifelong process of ever-growing faith development. Faith is not a static goal we attain but an unfolding journey of discovery and mystery. It is grounded in the daily tasks and relationships of our lives and comes full cycle into maturing expression and involvement with those same daily tasks and relationships.

Since *all* experience has the potential for learning, the division between sacred and secular fades away. In viewing life's experiences as God-given, and our capacity to take note and organize those experiences into meaningful frameworks as a gift of grace, our journey of lifelong learning is at every moment a sacred one. Whether the experience and struggle to make meaning of it are painful or joyful, the whole process is sacred. Whether the learning event takes place within a religious context or outside of one, the moment is God-given. Lifelong learning and the faith journey are one and the same.

A faith that is vibrant and alive cannot be taught. It is not passed on from an expert authority to a novice student. It must be owned by each individual in relationship to God. With more of the properties of a verb than a noun, faith is in the process of being created. It grows and develops its strength and richness as people go through the cycle of experiencing, reflecting, making meaning, and using the insights to guide their future lives.

IMPLICATIONS FOR ADULT RELIGIOUS EDUCATORS

When faith development is viewed as a transformative, creative unfolding of the whole person over a lifetime, the role of the religious educator is greatly expanded. Such a perspective suggests implications limited only by the creative imagination of practitioners. The following suggestions of applications to church-based learning groups are intended as a springboard to stimulate ideas for thoughtful and responsible experimentation. The resultant adult religious learning contributes to adult development.

Applications for Church-Based Learning Groups

I believe that "there is no better place to begin than with ourselves."[18] Leaders who are aware of their own ongoing faith journey and who are open in sharing of themselves help to create a safe environment for the learning of others. By refusing to take on the role of expert advisor set apart from the people, they relate to parishioners as companions on the way. Leaders and participants are at times both teachers and learners. All have life stories that are being written in their daily undertakings and all have expertise to struggle with their meanings.

Adult religious educators need to have knowledge about the characteristics of adult learners and how they learn. They must understand how to implement educational principles in their program design and group leadership. When educators are knowledgeable about adult learning methodology, groups are more likely to be dynamic, interdependent communities which attract people motivated to deepen their understanding of their call to be Christian.

The importance of attending to the learning processes happening within and among people in a group is as important to religious educators as is the subject matter. Helping people to get to know one another and feel welcome and comfortable in a study group is a critical step in setting the stage for the sharing and risk-taking that will follow. Chairs in a circle, a warm comfortable room (for example, a church parlor or a living room in a home instead of a sterile classroom), tea or coffee or juice available, friendly greetings, and calling people by name all set a tone for a collaborative and inviting experience.

Starting with group-building exercises that help people get to know one another and clarify expectations invites participants to share the responsibility for creating a positive learning environment. Discussion topics and activities using pairs, triads, and small groups can be interspersed with large group structures to vary the pace and promote increased safety for more personal sharing with a few people at a time.

Activities that appeal to a wide range of learning styles respect the variety present in the group. Strategies that access sight and hearing and other senses, body movement, feelings, critical thinking, and imagination engage the whole person. Logical, analytical, detailed thinking as well as metaphorical, symbolic, intuitive images invite both left-brain and right-brain participation. Discussion, silent meditation, music, poetry, inspirational readings, guided imagery, movement, journalling, visual aids (for example, flip charts, overheads, posters, artwork, films, photos, proverbs or sayings written out, signs posted), and drama can be used to provide a variety in design and resources; this assists individuals in staying focused and involved.

Kolb's cycle suggests a framework for the design of sessions. Beginning with *concrete experience*, people may think of an incident that has occurred in their life or there may be an activity which the group engages in which becomes the experience focusing their energy. Then the educator leads the group in reflecting on the experience. This is the phase of *reflective observation*. The reflection may be done individually through writing or quiet meditation, in pairs or small groups, or in the large group. Questions may guide the reflection. "What did you notice?" "What was going on?" "How did you feel?" "What were other people's reactions?"

Eventually the questions move people on to the theorizing or meaning-making phase, *abstract conceptualization*. "How do you account for that?" "What scripture passages speak to your experience?" "How does that fit in with other beliefs?" These kinds of questions help people generalize and begin to form theories or frameworks for understanding. Finally, the educator leads the group on to consider implications for future behavior, *active experimentation*. "How will this insight or belief affect your relationships at home or work?" "What will you do differently (or repeat) another time?" "How will you put this new knowledge or belief into practice?" "How will your life be different?" At times the experimenting may be prepared for by discussing the options in the group, considering obstacles to change, planning ahead, articulating resources and supports for change, or engaging in role-plays or imaginary rehearsal.

This planned implementation then becomes yet another experience for people to take note of and to reflect upon, in order to make sense of it, so that they will have increased knowledge to guide future action. Thus the cyclical nature of learning spins on like a wheel long after the group disbands. Religious educators who help parishioners become aware of this natural cycle of learning from everyday happenings empower adults by facilitating their getting in touch with a process which they themselves can continue to use intentionally.

These are a few suggestions of some implications for practice for applying adult education principles in a religious setting. Further reflection, conceptualization, and experimentation will continue to give birth to strategies and designs for faith learning experiences that transform and empower the individuals and communities in which religious educators minister.

Adult Religious Learning Contributes to Adult Development

Adult religious educators are in a position to help in people appreciate the sacredness of all of life. They can aid people in making connections between their daily lives and their spiritual meaning-making. Religious educators with a sense of ministry for both themselves and participants in learning groups are able to assist people in realizing that everyday tasks and relationships contain the seeds for learning and growth. Many adults are eager for help in linking their spiritual understandings to their everyday interactions and tasks. Faith development is not limited to Bible study groups or prayer meetings. It does not happen only once a week within the church walls. Faith matures as people live out the daily challenges of relationships and responsibilities that preoccupy them. The role of religious educators is to assist individuals in recognizing that, as they engage in these tasks and inter-actions, they learn to live intentionally grounded in their beliefs. The learning episode is a sacred encounter with themselves, others, the subject matter, and God. As religious educators of adults share a process of discovery, they empower others in their maturing faith journey and are at the same time enriched in their own personal faith development.

Adult learning in a religious context is more than simply ongoing learning of religious information and perspectives. It includes the development of adults as spiritual people.

DISCUSSION QUESTIONS

1. What ideas expressed in this chapter stand out for you?

2. Share something of your own faith journey thus far. .

3. How do you implement adult learning principles and conditions in the groups you lead?

4. What learning strategies and structures help people ground their spiritual understandings in their own experiences?

5. Share more ways religious adult educators can help adults develop a vision of the wholeness of their lives.

6. In your particular church setting, what can you realistically initiate within the next year to nurture a group of adults in their faith development?

NOTES

1. With a focus on the teacher, Maria Harris explicates a theology of teaching as sacrament. See Maria Harris, *Teaching and Religious Imagination* (San Francisco: Harper and Row, 1987), p. 21.

2. Ibid., p. 42.

3. Thomas Moore, *Care of the Soul* (New York: Harper Perennial, 1992). This book offers a guide for cultivating depth and sacredness in everyday life.

4. There are many excellent writings that express teachings by aboriginal elders and leaders about the unity and harmony of all life. Three are: Peter Knudtson and David Suzuki, *Wisdom of the Elders*

(Toronto: Stoddart, 1992); Jerry Mander, *In the Absence of the Sacred* (San Francisco: Sierra Club Books, 1991); Rupert Ross, *Dancing with a Ghost* (Markham, Ontario: Octopus Publishing Group, 1992).

5. John P. Miller, *The Holistic Curriculum* (Toronto: OISE Press, 1988), p. 3.

6. Portions of Bill Marrevee's unpublished manuscript are quoted in National Advisory Committee on Adult Education, *Adult Faith Adult Church* (National Office of Religious Education, Canadian Conference of Catholic Bishops, Ottawa, Ontario), pp. 34-35.

7. Stephen D. Brookfield, *Understanding and Facilitating Adult Learning* (San Francisco: Jossey-Bass, 1986).

8. Donald H. Brundage and Dorothy MacKeracher, *Adult Learning Principles and Their Application to Program Planning* (Toronto: OISE, 1980).

9. J. Roby Kidd, *How Adults Learn*, 2nd edition (New York: Association Press, 1973).

10. Malcolm S. Knowles, *Andragogy in Action* (New York: Jossey-Bass, 1984).

11. Robert Smith, *Learning How to Learn* (Milton Keynes, England: Open University Press, 1984).

12. Carl Rogers has had an immense impact on the fields of education and psychotherapy. See Carl Rogers, *Freedom to Learn for the 80's* (Columbus, Ohio: Merrill, 1983).

13. Brookfield, *Understanding and Facilitating Adult Learning*, p. 30.

14. Brundage and MacKeracher, *Adult Learning Principles and Their Application to Program Planning*, p. 102.

15. Smith, *Learning How to Learn*, p. 60.

16. Margaret Fisher Brillinger, "Helping Adults Learn," *Journal of Human Lactation* 6, 4, (December, 1990). pp. 15-18.

17. David A. Kolb, *Experiential Learning: Experience as the Source of Learning and Development* (Englewood Cliffs, N.J.: Prentice-Hall, 1984).

18. Brillinger, "Helping Adults Learn," p. 171.

ABOUT THE AUTHOR

Margaret Fisher Brillinger is Associate Instructor in the Department of Adult Education at The Ontario Institute for Studies in Education, Toronto, Ontario, Canada. She holds a Doctor of Education degree with a specialization in adult education from the University of Toronto. She is a consultant and educator for many professional organizations, churches, and agencies. She teaches continuing education courses for clergy at the Toronto School of Theology. As a clinical member and approved supervisor with the American Association for Marriage and Family Therapy, she also has a private counselling practice. Dr. Brillinger has written articles on marriage and family education and on adult learning and development.

PART II

THE MANY DIMENSIONS OF ADULT RELIGIOUS EDUCATION IN THE COMMUNITY

The dimensions of religious education for adults are as multifaceted as the occasions of growth throughout life. The constant changes and transitions that characterize living in a community provide countless opportunities for faith development. However, if adult religious education is to be successful, it must be sensitive to the local community that it serves. It is the community that provides the content, the needs, the issues and the interests for this evolving field. Some practitioners have asked how adult religious education can be responsive to a community. Within this part, some of the answers to this question are discussed.

Due to the fact that participation in adult religious education is voluntary and that programs require a responsiveness to the collective community, Maurice Taylor discusses the art and science of program planning in this specialized field. Through an overview of the current adult education literature on planning models, the foundation is set to examine a number of existing adult religious education programs and the planning process that was actually used. He suggests that by bridging the theory with realities of practice important lessons and insights can be drawn that may help practitioners in designing effective programs.

Using the framework of the ecumenical liturgical community, Frank Henderson describes how Christian people need to be invited and enabled to enter into full participation in worship. He posits that the liturgical formation for both clergy and adult lay people is intrinsically inadequate and requires some rethinking.

Based on the principles and methods of adult learning, he discusses the term critical thinking and its applicability to adult religious education in local church communities. The main argument of the chapter suggests that the concept of critical thinking has the potential for including both the affective and spiritual dimensions of liturgical experience.

Another important dimension of adult religious education is that it takes place within a cultural context that is community based. Gregory Dunwoody outlines how the content, the methods and even the language of adult religious education are influenced by culture. Using Native communities, especially the Ojibway and Cree peoples as a case study, he illustrates why adult religious education must take into account the cultural factors of any particular community. In addition, he discusses the practical considerations that apply to other cultural groupings such as the African-Americans/Canadians, Hispanics, Vietnamese, Koreans and Ukrainians.

Many types of activities, events and people can precipitate a unifying force within a community. Pastoral counseling, for example, is one of those forces. In her chapter, Ruth Wright presents a view of pastoral counseling as part of the healing ministry of the church which must be shared among clerics and laity. She describes the church's role in healing and distinguishes between pastoral counseling and pastoral care. This is followed by a description of the parochial context. As well, she portrays the development of community programs from a practical perspective.

Intertwined throughout each of the chapters is the common thread of community responsiveness. Each author has chosen some dimension of adult religious education and illustrated how an activity, specific interest or event can be better integrated in the community. Whether it be liturgical formation or pastoral counselling, adult religious education has the potential to relate to the various communities in which it takes place.

1. PROGRAM PLANNING IN ADULT RELIGIOUS EDUCATION

Maurice C. Taylor

At a number of recent conferences, the topic of program planning has been an engaging conversation among adult religious educators. Whether in a study group or at a coffee break, educators seem to voice a common set of questions. Where did you start in the planning process? What kinds of needs assessment did you use? How did you deal with the content versus process dilemma? What was your attendance like? Did you use the standard form of evaluation? What's your formula for success? What's a good resource to read on this topic? Underlying these practical questions is the fact that most facilitators find the activity of planning religious educational programs for adults to be a complex decision making process.

With the many types of adult religious education in the community now increasing in size and diversity, these kinds of questions signal a need to further discuss the art and science of program planning in the specialized field of adult religious education. There are three purposes to this chapter. In the first section, an overview of the current adult education literature on planning models is presented. This review integrates and synthesizes the recent thinking and research in the area of interest.

The next section profiles a number of existing adult religious education programs with a particular focus on the planning process that was actually used. In this discussion, the reader gets a glimpse of what is really happening in the field. It describes the various combinations of steps used in moving a program idea to the actual implementation phase. At the same time, these profiles provide a framework for understanding the strengths and limitations of the information presented in the literature review. With the many dimensions and facets of adult religious education growing in complexity, these case studies can also serve to anchor us in the day-to-day realities of what is actually doable in community practice.

The chapter concludes with some important lessons drawn from the literature and actual practice that program planners may find useful as they continue their work. By bridging the theory which is presented in the first section with the realities of practice, the reader is left with a message that supporting adults in their faith development now requires a very different approach than in the past.

SURVEYING THE ADULT EDUCATION LITERATURE ON PROGRAM PLANNING MODELS

Anyone thumbing through the literature on program planning will find a multitude of books, chapters and practical guides written about the process of planning programs for adult learners. For example, in a recent analysis of the program planning literature, Thomas Sork and John Buskey examined over 93 publications which contained explicit or implicit planning models.[1] In referring to this seminal work, a six-step basic model may be useful to organize the discussion of the process and to illustrate the most common planning logic found in the literature. The six steps are: (a) analyze the planning context (b) assess needs, (c) develop program objectives, (d) formulate instructional plan, (e) formulate administrative plan, and (f) design a program evaluation plan.

Before embarking on any discussion on the basic elements of planning, it is important to define the term planning model. A planning model is a tool used to help understand and to bring order to a complex decision-making process. The typical planning model consists of a set of steps or elements that suggests decisions that must be made and dependent relationships that exist between the various decisions.[2] Although most program planning models in adult education help systemize the work of a practitioner, they often oversimplify the process as it occurs in practice. In addition, it is important to recognize that the literature on program planning is largely normative. This means that much of the written information on this topic consists of descriptions of how planning *should* be done rather than descriptions of *how* planning is done.

How to Plan Systematically

The first step in designing effective and relevant educational programs is to analyze the planning context. This simply means that programs are planned within certain institutions and organizations that have historical characteristics, philosophical concerns, and cultures that affect the planning process.[3] By analyzing the context it is possible to identify the internal and external factors that should be taken into account during the planning. For example, if an organization is about to begin a three-year restructuring process, the flow of authority and communication is an important internal factor to be considered. As well, if an institution is viewed by the community at large as delivering accountable and innovative services, this external factor can be used in making decisions about the planning milieu.

Connected to the analysis of the planning context is the importance of understanding the client system or the potential group of learners.[4] An analysis of the client system involves collecting baseline information about those individuals who are eligible for the attention of the program planner. By obtaining relevant information about the potential group of learners—such as cultural background, history of participation in education or social affiliations—it becomes possible to determine who is and who is not eligible for the attention of the planner. Collecting this type of information enables the needs assessment to be properly designed.

A second step entrenched in the planning literature is referred to as needs assessment. Some of the literature suggests that it is useful to think of educational needs as gaps between current and desired proficiencies. Adopting this discrepancy definition of needs means that valued judgments are an integral part of the needs assessment process, because identifying needs requires the specification of a more desirable condition or state of affairs.[5] Some of the major needs assessment procedures to determine a present condition include: self-assessment inventories, interest check lists, observation guides, reviewing organizational records, task analysis, and obtaining opinions of experts. The wide variety of methods for educational needs assessments makes it difficult to choose those that are best in a particular instance. However, the combination of methods selected should complement one another. This occurs when perspectives of both experts and potential participants are included. For example, Alan Knox reports:

> Another approach to selection of procedures for gathering information about educational needs occurred when Dorothy Olsson prepared to conduct her first adult religious education class after years as a participant. Informal conversations with congregation members identified some topics of widespread interest, but Dorothy felt that those topics might have reflected familiarity with past programs. A religious education conference provided a convenient opportunity to get opinions from two additional sources. Conference speakers and planners identified some emerging trends and issues likely to kindle enthusiasm. Experienced instructors from similar congregations told Dorothy about topics and discussion materials that had generated a large and spirited response. Dorothy selected a program topic mentioned by peers and leaders at the conference as

well as by members of her congregation who seemed likely to participate.[6]

The next step in the planning process is the development of the program objectives. Although there is some debate in the literature about the specificity of program objectives, they should flow from the needs that have been identified. Program objectives are actually statements of the anticipated results of the program. Having objectives of an educational activity made explicit accomplishes a number of purposes. When objectives are known, they can help to shape the format, provide a description of the activity, clarify the thinking of planners and learners, and provide a sense of unity.[7] There are several types of objectives. One is a statement of the expected outcome or change in behavior. Another type is objectives stated as principles that guide the process. A third type is facilitative, that is objectives that affect the format of the design. Objectives can be broad in scope or take on a much narrower focus such as outlines of the results of one specific workshop or conference. The literature also suggests that there are two important purposes for developing program objectives. One of the purposes is to provide concrete guidelines for further program development. A second purpose is to serve as benchmarks for measuring the progress and achievements of a program.

The fourth step in program planning is formulating an instructional plan. This plan may include preparing instructional objectives, selecting and ordering content, designing the instructional process, selecting appropriate resources, and determining evaluation procedures. Instructional objectives are different from program objectives. In formulating an instructional plan, these objectives describe the outcomes or results of a specific learning segment or activity and are written from the perspective of the individual learner.

In terms of ordering content, William Tracey provides some general guidelines that may be helpful to instructors. First, provide an overall framework of the content for learners to assist them in organizing their learning. Second, try to start with material that may be familiar to the learner so that their experience and background can become part of the learning process. Third, where appropriate, provide practical exercises or applications as part of each learning segment.[8] Determining the content goes hand-in-hand with selecting the instructional process which is described in much more detail in other chapters of the book. Although there is no best way of assisting adults to learn, some factors that influence the choices around instructional strategies include: previous experience of the instructor, background of the adult learner, instructional objectives, time, equipment, and space.

Thomas Sork and Rosemary Caffarella describe the fifth step in program planning as the formulation of an administrative plan.[9] One of the major functions of this step is to address the administrative tasks and details that are important to a well-designed program—for example, advanced publicity and financing. According to E.J. Boone, marketing in adult education, which is part of publicity, means gaining acceptance of, consensus upon, or participation in any given educational venture.[10] Successful marketing of the plans of action and the overall program is dependent upon time, location, and costs to the participants. No formula will guarantee success. The literature also suggests that there are three basic costs attached to most educational programs: development costs, delivery costs, and evaluation costs.

The final step in a model for program planning is called the design of an evaluation plan. Continuous evaluation is an essential function of any program in order to provide information about: (a) how well the program is working, and (b) what can be done to improve it. Evaluation should answer two questions: "How effective is the program?"; this is a summative evaluation question, and also, "What can be done to improve the program?";

this is a formative evaluation question. The summative evaluation function focuses on the results of a program and is usually carried out at the conclusion of the program, whereas formative program evaluation emphasizes further development, and should be conducted periodically throughout the implementation of the program. Answers to formative evaluation questions are intended to be used for improving the program as it is in progress.[11]

Once it has been decided what to evaluate, the next set of decisions include determining the evaluation design, planning the collection of data, specifying data analysis procedures, and establishing evaluation criteria. More recently there has been a focus on not only using evaluation information to examine successful programs but also the failures in program design or programs that have been unsuccessful.

HOW IS PROGRAM PLANNING DONE IN THE FIELD?

As can be seen from the previous discussion, the adult education literature in program planning is largely normative. Because of this limitation, there is a need to find out how planning is done in some of the existing programs in the field. In an attempt to look at a variety of educational environments, I asked a number of experts in adult religious education to describe what actually occurs in terms of the planning process.[12] This characteristic links all of the case studies. Using a common set of guiding questions, each expert wrote a synopsis of their perceptions of the process. The following profiles are based on the notes sent to me and include: Gospel Table Talk; Touch the Poor, Touch God; Parents Preparing Children for First Communion; The Gospel of Mark: Video Program; and Loyola's Institute for Ministry Extension Program.

Gospel Table Talk

Gospel Table Talk was born from the Lenten Series conducted in four parishes in the Northside Deanery of the Diocese of Antigonish during Lent of 1989. It was the expressed wish of a number of the Lenten participants that a similar process be continued on a regular basis. The Northside Adult Faith Office sponsored the program which continues today. The purpose of the program is to facilitate faith enrichment and sharing and to develop a sense of the "domestic church." The program is designed for interested adults who are willing to make a commitment to be part of a neighborhood home reflection group and to offer their homes as a home of hospitality for Gospel Table Talk. The program started off with home meetings one hour once a month, with the day and time scheduled by the group themselves. A general gathering once every four to six weeks occurs. As the program evolved the participants were willing to make a weekly commitment in preparation for Sunday's eucharists. The purpose of the general meeting is intended to provide a "gathering experience" for all involved in the program. It brings together the faithful from the various parishes and provides an experience of the broader church community. It is also a forum to respond to the themes, issues, concerns, and questions of the Christian faith which surfaced at the time of shared reflection during the Gospel Table Talk sessions.

The title Gospel Table Talk was chosen to highlight the liturgy of the word as living eucharist in daily life. The facilitators invited interested persons to form a group and used the guidelines as outlined in the Catechetical Process for Reflection on the Gospel. The director of the Adult Faith Office is also informed of the group's progress, especially around the issues, concerns and questions of faith. Each leader of Gospel Table Talk is trained in the "how to" of the catechetical process. Initially seven group leaders were trained and participants numbered thirty-five. New leaders are prepared as the group evolves and the need arises. The gospel background (in biblical language, the exegesis) for each gospel is prepared from the Adult Faith Office and forwarded to each home leader.

As the group grows and develops, the second stage of preparation in training is provided for the home leader or facilitators.

Touch the Poor, Touch God

This thirteen-day program provides Catholic and non-Catholic university students from campus ministry communities with a direct experience with the Mexican poor and with Central American refugees in their daily struggle for survival. The need for the program arose from the adult students themselves who wanted to have an experience in a less developed country but did not have the language, the support, nor an extended period of time. The goal of the program is to have students come to a deeper awareness of the reality of poverty, hunger, and oppressive structures. It is intended to help young adults discover ways of acting that bring about change, and it is intended that in the process, they would become empowered to return to their communities to work with the poor at the local level.

Once the need was identified, it was brought to the Student Association Executive and to the Campus Ministry Advisory Committee. These groups helped decide what such a program should have: hands-on experience with the poor, opportunity for small group interaction, a community experience of living and praying together, and leaders who knew both the Latin and North American worlds. The Cuernavaca Center for Dialog on Development in Cuernavaca, Mexico, was then chosen as the vehicle for the experiential learning program.

The program is coordinated by North Americans who have roots in Latin America. They set up the encounters that form the backbone of the program. Much of the student's time is spent visiting people in their environments—shanty towns, indigenous people, mountain villages, parish churches, people's homes, cooperatives, and grass roots medical clinics. The program moves from personal encounter of the poor where they live; to meeting poor people who are agents of change within their local community; to people who have collectively gathered to bring about change; to the connection with North American life and reality; and then to a time of synthesis, analysis, and looking forward.

The program incorporates two levels of teaching strategies. At the first level is personal story telling and interaction with the story teller; this involves small group processing and large group reflection. At the second level participants relate what they have heard, along with critical analysis and action plans, using both small and large group processes. Every day time is also given for personal reflection, for journalling, for personal interaction with the culture, for reading, and for discussing topics of interest to the individual. Before the program begins, there is a small bibliography given to the students with suggested books, movies and such for them to read before or after the event. However, it is through the story telling, reflections, and dialogue with the poor themselves that each participant is challenged to grow in awareness, in faith, and in a commitment to become involved in change.

The program pays for itself. The participants are charged a fee for the program which covers their travel, lodging and food costs. In most cases, the participants fund raise individually or through the community as a way of getting the money to attend. In terms of evaluation, both oral and written types are conducted. During the program a small group of students is elected to represent the group. They participate in shaping the program in response to the needs of the group and the issues and questions that arise on site. The program is also evaluated at the national advisory committee level.

Parents Preparing Children for First Communion

When it came time to prepare children for first communion in a Native community of two hundred people, a new process was introduced which prepared the parents, who in turn prepared their own children. The need for the first communion program was identified by a number of the mothers in the community. The basic goal selected by the parents was sacramental preparation. As the program developed, the facilitator—who is involved in the development of the local church—also added the following goals: building the sense of co-responsibility within the broad faith community, building up the knowledge base of the parents and in particular their understanding of the eucharist, reestablishing the sense of parental responsibility for the faith development of children, and enriching the liturgical life of the community.

The facilitator meets with the parents every two weeks for a period of three months to review materials and progress, prepare liturgies, consider the meaning of the eucharist, and discuss any other issues which arise during the meetings. Seven families participated in this program. Attendance at the meetings, which were held in a room attached to the church, varied from three to five. Four special liturgies were conducted on Sundays during the program. Mothers worked from the copies of a teacher's manual and the children had workbooks adapted from Southern materials.

Meetings with the parents followed a varying format. They always included prayer and discussion of progress made, difficulties encountered, and ideas for future sessions. Written materials were kept to a minimum. Sometimes, however, climate-setting sheets were used to start discussion or for personal reflection prior to smaller group work. The Bible was used as a basis for many of the discussions. Liturgies were planned, roles assigned, and bread was broken together on one of the evenings. The predominant teaching technique used was the group discussion, structured over an evening according to a predetermined plan. The different sessions took on an inquiring nature that followed the natural path of people's interest.

Throughout the program, a number of obstacles were overcome. When the meetings first started some parents felt uneasy undertaking the task of sacramental preparation, which was formerly considered to be that of a religious. This uncertainty resulted in a lack of confidence when taking on the leadership role. At times, the facilitator also felt he had a limited understanding of the sacrament, which meant that more time had to be given to the preparation of meetings. Another barrier that affected participation in the program was the discomfort of some of the parents who were prevented from receiving the eucharist because of their common law marital status.

The Gospel of St. Mark: Video Program

This program consisted of sixteen half-hour weekly presentations on public television. It was produced by the Adult Learning Centre in conjunction with the Archdiocesan Communications Centre. The audience was made up of seventy groups of people who met in their homes one hour before the television presentation. These groups were mainly Anglican, Protestant, and Catholic. Each participant received a study pamphlet with the readings and questions covered during the presentation. The program was repeated three times weekly—once in the morning and twice in the evening. At the end of all presentations the facilitator would come on live to answer questions from the various groups. The need for the program was determined simply by the fact that so few people were knowledgeable about the Bible. The goal was to enable people to see the gospel of Mark in a new light, as well as to be enriched through the sharing of their own insights. Each program covered several paragraphs of Mark's gospel. In a two-year period, sixteen programs covered the entire gospel .

The teaching technique was basically that of groups meeting in homes reflecting on a selected portion of

Mark's gospel one hour before the television presentation, which then covered the same materials the group had reflected upon. The television time was free because the educational station was owned by a consortium of public institutions including the Archdiocesan Communications Centre. The Centre produced the program free of charge. The only expenses were the printing of the pamphlet and the time that went into the production work.

The program continued for four years, covering the gospel of Mark and the gospel of John. At the end of this period the television station was taken over by the province of Alberta. Only an informal evaluation was conducted from the various study groups and other people who listened to the program. Judging by the number of people who had asked questions on the live program, the facilitators felt that it was reaching a large audience. During its four years on the air, one appraisal of the program was that insufficient time was spent organizing the local reflection groups and keeping in touch with them.

Loyola's Institute for Ministry, Extension Program (LIMEX)

The Resurrection Centre which runs Loyola's Institute for Ministry, Extension Program (LIMEX), is involved in the education, formation, and training of lay people for adult ministry in all aspects of parish and church life. A four-member staff is committed to the structuring of faith communities with a special focus on the parish community, the Catholic education community, and communities representing the marginalized.

With a new generation of ministers and educators, many of them lay people taking up the challenge of church leadership, training is essential. A need was identified in order to provide these new ministers with an informed and contemporary theological vision, professional competence, and practical ministerial skills. In cooperation with Resurrection Centre and the Diocese of Hamilton, Ontario, Loyola's Institute for Ministry in

New Orleans responded to the needs of ministry and education personnel who have limited access to educational resources by offering an extensive ten courses over the span of three and a half years. It is a continuing education program in pastoral studies.

The LIMEX program's educational philosophy and curriculum are based on sound principles of adult education and theological reflection. The two main principles that have shaped the program are: the learner is central, and ministry always takes place within a context. Each individual has the task of integrating by means of a reflection process the four aspects of the overall context of ministry, tradition, culture, institution and personal experience. "Ministry in context" provides students with a model of theoretical reflection based on the work of Bernard Lonergan.

The Institute for Ministry has established a contractual relationship with Resurrection Centre which functions as a sponsoring agency. Loyola has appointed a staff member as the administrator of the extension studies. He has participated in a facilitator's training program and acts as the link between the Institute and Resurrection Centre. The liaison is responsible for recruiting participants, coordinating and administrating the program, and recruiting facilitators who are ultimately responsible for conducting the ten courses over a period of three to four years. Loyola's Institute for Ministry Education Program is a graduate level program of study in education for ministry. Individual courses are comprised of ten class meetings, three hours each, in which participants engage in group process. Within the learning group academics are put in dialogue with ministerial practice. Preparation for each class usually involves six to eight hours of reading and assignments. Full participation in the group's activities and reading evaluation is required. Papers, examinations, or other work assigned for evaluation are determined by the individual's sponsoring agencies.

The major barrier in this program was the securing of an endorsement in support of the local Ordinary and diocese and the personnel in the diocese who are responsible for adult religious education. This barrier happily became a distinctive asset in terms of support provided.

THE REALITIES OF PRACTICE—LESSONS TO BE LEARNED

In the preceding section five different programs have been sketched out to provide the reader with a sense of how planning was actually done. By bridging the "theory," which was presented in the first section, with the actual realities of practice some important insights and lessons can be learned. The following discussion examines the various program profiles in light of the literature on program planning.

Lesson 1—Build in Time to Understand the Planning Context

Although not explicitly described in these scenarios, the planners have made an attempt to analyze the planning context and client system. In some cases internal and external factors were taken into account during the planning. For example, in the Gospel Table Talk program, the flow of communication between the group leaders and the director of the Northside Adult Faith Office was considered to be an important internal factor. In the LIMEX program, which is based at the Resurrection Centre, the mission of the organization affected how the planning proceeded. The fact that the Centre was committed to the concept of collaboration in ministry meant that the staff members worked closely with the major ministries of the local dioceses, and this was a contextual factor that influenced the direction of the planning process. In an effort to undertake some type of client system analysis for the Parents Preparing Children for First Communion program, informal results revealed that the group preferred not to use a lot of written materials in the program. This characteristic had important implications for later steps of the planning design. Although researchers have helped us develop a rudimentary understanding of why people do and do not participate in programs, identification of all the planning implications of specific contextual factors or client characteristics is still difficult.

Lesson 2—Needs Assessments Are the Cornerstones of a Good Program

All of the programs described used some type of needs assessment. In the case of the Gospel of St. Mark Video Program, the observation by Learning Centre staff that so few people were knowledgeable about the Bible fuelled the need to change the situation. In Touch the Poor, Touch God, the continuous requests from young adult students reaffirmed the need for such an experiential program. In Gospel Table Talk, the actual participants from a previous pilot-type of program expressed the need that a similar process be continued on a regular basis. In the Parents Preparing Children for First Communion, mothers in the Native community identified the need. It is interesting to note that sophisticated procedures to determine the present condition based on data acquired through questionnaires, tests and self-assessment instruments were not actually used in these programs.

Although the centrality of needs assessment and the various procedures in the planning literature are undisputed, there appears to be a growing awareness among researchers and practitioners, who urge a revision in thinking about the importance of needs assessment to effective educational planning. Practitioners argue that they rarely have time to conduct a formal needs assessment. More often than not they justify offering programs based on potential demand. Such is the case in the LIMEX program. With the new generation of ministers and educators, many of them lay people taking up the challenge of church leadership, there was a potential demand for training. As Thomas Sork has suggested, it may be time to revise planning theory so that it takes into account more of the contextual circumstances confronted by practitioners—circumstances that limit the practical utility of needs assessment and offer other legitimate means of justifying and focusing programs.[13]

Lesson 3—Objectives Help To Clarify for All Program Participants

As can be seen from the program descriptions, the level of specificity of the statement of objectives varies. In Gospel Table Talk, Touch the Poor, and Parents Preparing Children for First Communion, the program objectives are broad in scope. In all three cases the objectives flowed from the needs that had been identified and were presented in the format that captured the desired state of affairs. In these examples, the objectives had meaning for all parties involved, including the facilitator, the organizational staff, and the participants.

There is some question in the literature as to whether or not program objectives should be fixed entities, determined prior to the start of a program. Some authors raise the issue of whether or not it is always important or even possible to identify expected outcomes before an educational program begins. In following this rationale, program objectives can be seen as somewhat open-ended so that unanticipated but important outcomes of the program can be noted. Stephen Brookfield suggests that if objectives are stated primarily in behavforial terms, then only instrumental or technical learning is supported and emancipatory or reflected learning is ignored.[14]

Lesson 4—Encourage Negotiation between Facilitators and Learners

In the program descriptions, the reader finds different approaches in formulating the instructional plan—the larger the audience the more specific the plan. There is evidence in the program sketches that there is no best way of assisting adults to learn. Through a variety of methodologies, content, and equipment, the design of instruction can be placed on a continuum with systematic approaches at one end and artistic or creative approaches at the other. One issue that has surfaced in the program planning literature centers on how adult education should design the actual instructional process. There seems to be a constant tension between the content of instruction and the process of instruction. Should we as adult educators primarily be facilitators of the learning process with the emphasis on helping learners become more self-directed in their learning endeavors? Or should we be more content-oriented and thus be largely concerned with whether learners gain new knowledge and skills or whether they change their values or attitudes in some way? In adult religious education this scenario is very much the same. Based on the program sketches, this tension seems to be relaxed by two factors—through the expressed needs of the participants and the previous training and experience of the program facilitator.

Lesson 5—Administrative and Instructional Plans Go Hand in Hand

In the program sketches there are three good examples that illustrate the advantages of formulating an administrative plan. In planning the gospel of Mark video programs, a partnership was formed among the Adult Learning Centre, the Archdiocesan Communications Centre and the TV station. Although all the details of the responsibilities of the different partners are not fully described in the sketches, it is evident that administrative tasks such as publicity, program financing, coordination of the study groups, materials production, and facilitation of the live feedback session were shared. In the case of the LIMEX program a contractual agreement was established between Loyola's Institute for Ministry and the Resurrection Centre. Through this agreement, administrative tasks were clearly defined. The liaison person was responsible for recruiting participants, coordinating and administrating the program, and recruiting facilitators. This liaison person was also involved in the facilitators' training program before the launching of the LIMEX, which enhanced the overall planning process. In designing the program Touch the Poor, Touch God, one factor that contributed to its success was the administrative link that was established with the Cuernavaca Center for Dialog on Development in Mexico. Important program components, such as organizing the field experiences, and program details, such as lodging and food for the participants, were all planned in advance.

An issue that seems to come up regularly in the program planning literature is the market-driven practice of program planning. When adult educators are expected to operate programs on a cost-recovery or profit making basis, the need to fill classrooms or workshops with paying customers instead of emphasizing the educational needs of the citizenry at large tends to become the major force that drives programs. In adult religious education, programs seem to be driven by educational needs as opposed to economics.

Lesson 6—Take a Stance on Evaluation Early in the Planning Process

In terms of designing a program evaluation plan what we find in the program sketches are a range of ideas about what evaluation is and how it should be done. Although little attention was given to determining the evaluation design, planning the collection of data, and specifying data analysis procedures, there is a clear indication in each of the programs that various formative and summative evaluations were conducted. For instance, in Gospel Table Talk, as the program evolved and improved the need to provide additional training for the home leaders or facilitators was identified and addressed. Using a slightly different approach, an elected group of young adult students acted as a clarifying team throughout the Touch the Poor, Touch God program. In Parents Preparing Children for First Communion, a review of materials and the progress of the program was done every two weeks for a period of three months. In the Gospel of St. Mark Video Program, the summative evaluation indicated that more time should have been spent organizing the local reflection groups. In the LIMEX program, papers, examinations, readings and other assigned works were used to determine whether gains had been made in knowledge or skill levels.

Some authorities in adult education have raised the question as to the value of the whole evaluation process. The assumption that program evaluation needs to be systematic and precise has also been disputed, as has the assumption that quantitative data are preferable in demonstrating the value and worth of a program. As Stephen Brookfield points out, the very nature of adult education programs calls for alternative evaluation strategies such as the more naturalistic approaches.[15] The program sketches described in this chapter seem to support this approach.

Looking Forward

Recently the Canadian Conference of Catholic Bishops published a report entitled *Pathways to Faithfulness: Developing Structures Which Support Catechetical Ministry with Adults.* Threaded throughout the document is the clear message that there is an increasing awareness and commitment to supporting adults as they mature in faith. However, a call is also made to adult religious educators to take charge of certain challenges, such as the need for more effective organizing and support for this ministry. In describing planning for pastoral action, the report further asks us to consider certain key questions, such as: Who are the adults in our context? What are our goals and motivations for working with them? What principles, guidelines and approaches are appropriate for working with adults? What is the content? What models will meet the needs of a diverse adult population? How can these efforts be implemented, coordinated and evaluated? What human and material resources are needed for the enterprise?[16] In some respects, these penetrating questions seem to parallel the program planning steps just described in this chapter. They also seem to reflect a similar line of inquiry used by the five adult religious education experts whose actual process of program planning has been outlined earlier in this chapter. If there is one message in all of this it may be that to continue our work in supporting adults in their faith development now requires a more systematic approach than in the past.

DISCUSSION QUESTIONS

1. If you were to draw the program planning process in a flow chart, what would it look like?

2. What needs assessment procedures are most suitable to your own situation or environment?

3. Would you have planned any of the five programs described in the chapter differently? Why?

4. What is your stance on program evaluation?

5. Use a metaphor to describe your understanding of the program planning process.

NOTES

1. Thomas Sork and John Buskey, "A Descriptive and Evaluative Analysis of Program Planning Literature, 1950 to 1983," *Adult Education Quarterly* 36, no. 2 (1986), pp. 86-96.

2. Thomas Sork and Rosemary Caffarella, "Planning Programs for Adults," in 1990 *Handbook of Adult and Continuing Education*, ed. S. Merriam and P. Cunningham (San Francisco: Jossey-Bass, 1989), p. 234. This book is an excellent source for someone just beginning in the field of adult religious education.

3. Huey Long, *Adult and Continuing Education: Responding to Change* (New York: Teachers College Press, 1983).

4. Wayne Schroeder, "Typology of Adult Learning Systems," in *Building an Effective Adult Enterprise*, ed. J. Peters and Associates (San Francisco: Jossey-Bass, 1980).

5. Sork and Caffarella, *Planning Programs for Adults*, p. 237.

6. Alan Knox, *Helping Adults Learn* (San Francisco: Jossey-Bass Publishers, 1986), pp. 60-61.

7. Cyril Houle, *The Design of Education* (San Francisco: Jossey-Bass, 1972), pp. 137-143. This work is still referred to almost twenty-five years after its first publication.

8. William Tracey, *Designing Training and Development Systems* (New York: AMACOM, 1984).

9. Sork and Caffarella, *Planning Programs for Adults*, p. 240.

10. E.J. Boone, *Developing Programs in Adult Education* (Englewood Cliffs, NJ: Prentice-Hall, 1985), p. 157.

11. Edwin Simpson, "Program Development: A Model" in *Materials and Methods in Adult and Continuing Education*, ed. C. Klevins (Los Angeles: Klevens Publications, 1982), p. 97.

12. The author wishes to acknowledge the exemplary works of Sheila O'Handley, Anne Shore, Peter Hart, Jack Spicer, and Frank Ruetz. Their untiring efforts in designing and implementing adult religious education programs have been outstanding.

13. Thomas Sork, "Yellow Brick Road or Great Dismal Swamp: Pathways to Objectives and Program Planning" in *Proceedings of the 27th Annual Adult Education Research Conference* (Syracuse, N.Y.: Syracuse University Press, 1986).

14. Stephen Brookfield, *Understanding and Facilitating Adult Learning.* (San Francisco: Jossey-Bass, 1986).

15. Ibid.

16. Canadian Conference of Catholic Bishops, *Pathways to Faithfulness: Developing Structures Which Support Catechetical Ministry with Adults.* (Ottawa, Ont.: National Office of Religious Education, 1993), p. 53. This resource document can be used with both small and large groups in numerous types of training situations.

ABOUT THE AUTHOR

Maurice C. Taylor, an Associate Professor of Adult Education at the University of Ottawa, has worked in the field of adult literacy and basic skills training with the voluntary, business, community college, and university sectors. Author of many national and international literacy publications, he has collaborated on projects with the National Literacy Secretariat, the Movement for Canadian Literacy, World Literacy of Canada, and the Commonwealth Association for the Education Training of Adults. He has also acted in an administrative and advisory capacity to a number of national voluntary associations such as the Canadian Conference of Catholic Bishops.

2. IMPROVING LITURGICAL FORMATION THROUGH CRITICAL THINKING

J. Frank Henderson

Christian worship or liturgy calls for the full participation of the worshippers. This was a principle of the Reformation, and today it is accepted by most churches. The following words, though enunciated by the Second Vatican Council of the Roman Catholic Church, are widely endorsed in the ecumenical liturgical community:

> The Church earnestly desires that all the faithful be led to that full, conscious and active participation in liturgical celebration called for by the very nature of the liturgy. Such participation by the Christian people...is their right and duty by reason of their baptism.
>
> In the reform and promotion of the liturgy, this full and active participation by all the people is the aim to be considered before all else. For it is the primary and indispensable source from which the faithful are to derive their true Christian spirit.[1]

Christian women, men, and children need to be invited and enabled to enter into lives of full participation in worship. The term *liturgical formation* is used to refer to the many ways in which people are helped to enter more and more deeply into the liturgy. This is a lifelong task, need, and opportunity. It is my threefold thesis here that (a) liturgical formation for clergy and adult lay people, as it is typically carried out today, is intrinsically inadequate, (b) liturgical formation would be vastly improved if it were conducted using principles and methods of the approach to adult learning that is called *critical thinking*;[2]

110

and (c) that critical thinking is generally applicable to adult religious education in local church communities.

FORMATION FOR FULL PARTICIPATION IN THE LITURGY

In order to appreciate the needs of individuals and communities for liturgical formation, it is first necessary to consider the fuller meaning of liturgical participation. The "full, active and conscious participation" in liturgical celebrations that is the goal of all churches is a rich concept that embraces several dimensions or levels. It begins with our external actions during worship: what we say, sing, and do. It then includes our internal appropriation of the meaning and consequences of these actions: we understand and mean what we say, sing and do, and commit ourselves to live accordingly. Participation reaches out to signify as well the communion with other worshippers into which we enter by worshipping together, and the communion with worshippers and other persons which comes by living out the meaning of our corporate worship, for example, by ministering with those in need. It implies further the life of the church that we are becoming through these acts of communion in worship and ministry. Finally, participation names the communion with God that we experience in all of these ways.

Based on this understanding of participation, liturgical formation includes far more than cognitive knowledge and certain practical skills. It has to do with the affective dimensions of human life, with spirituality, and with ministry. It has to do with appreciating and living out the connections between worship and unemployment, poverty, family, AIDS, abortion, land claims, and immigration—to name only a few social issues.

Liturgical celebrations themselves are the primary mode of liturgical formation. They accomplish this to the extent that they are exemplary and life-giving. In addition, aspects of liturgy are considered in religious education programs for children and youth, and in continuing education offerings for adult lay people. Liturgy is included in the curricula of most theological schools, and in the continuing education of clergy. It is a responsibility of pastoral ministers and those involved in religious education to educate or form their parishioners with respect to liturgy in order to lead them to the "full, active and conscious participation" spoken of above.

The quality of the liturgical formation that is being carried out in the churches may be assessed by the quality of the liturgical celebrations—Sunday services, for example—that people actually experience. This varies widely, of course, and there are many churches where the liturgy is above average or very good. In others, however, liturgical experience is mediocre or even poor. It is neither inclusive nor life-giving; it has little to do with daily living; it is not transformative. In places there is a new concern for externals: for "liturgical correctness." There is a renewed clericalism, and hence the increased exclusion of lay people; the latter are expected to be more and more passive. There is a lack of spiritual depth.

The causes of poor liturgies are many and complex. The one factor that will be considered here, however, is that of liturgical formation: its assumptions, goals, methods, and approaches. Based on my own experience of teaching liturgy in a variety of institutional and non-institutional settings and with students from a variety of churches, I have concluded that traditional ways of carrying out liturgical formation are intrinsically inadequate, and that new approaches are required. The traditional ways can be compared with pedagogy; the new approaches required draw upon but differ slightly from andragogy.

Pedagogy

Liturgy courses in theological schools, as well as continuing education courses and events for laity, too often are conducted using methods that are referred to as pedagogical. Such courses try to convey a body of knowledge about liturgy from the teacher, who is the authority, to the students, who are relatively passive. They approach the subject in an abstract manner, and give little place to experience. They consider liturgy from the outside rather than from the inside. Cognitive dimensions are stressed, though practical skills sometimes are taught as well. Personal appropriation, integration of liturgy and daily living, and the place of liturgy in one's overall spirituality generally are neglected. Critique of the teacher's presentation is seldom welcomed, and alternatives to present views and practices are rarely considered.

The pedagogical approach is widely considered to be inappropriate for adults, regardless of the subject matter. This approach also runs counter to the primary mode of liturgical formation, the experience of worship itself. Thus, liturgy is first of all an experience, it is communal and participatory; it is embodied, affective and spiritual as well as cognitive. An ancient method of liturgical formation, which finds increasing favor today, is called mystagogy: reflection on high points of liturgical experience after they have occurred, and education regarding their meaning and significance.

Andragogy

Some continuing education programs for adult lay people use the adult learning approach called andragogy. Yet this does not entirely meet the needs of a comprehensive program of liturgical formation either.[3] Certainly, the assumption "that adults possess a reservoir of experiences that affect how they perceive the world and that represent an important source of material for curriculum development and learning activities"[4] seems valid and highly applicable to liturgical formation. Adults generally have years of Sunday worship experiences to build upon; to neglect this is tragic.

Stephen Brookfield, however, questions three other assumptions of andragogy, namely (a) that adults generally are self-directed; (b) that adults are aware of their learning needs because of their own life experiences; and (c) that adults are "competency-based" or "performance-centered" in that they wish to apply newly acquired skills or knowledge to their own lives. He suggests that self-directedness is, in fact, a rare quality that may be absent in members of many cultures and subcultures. The second and third assumptions, Brookfield says,

> can easily lead to a technological interpretation of learning that is highly reductionist. Underlying these tenets is a view of learning that could lead practitioners to equate the sum total of adult learning with instrumental learning; that is, learning how to perform at an improved level of competence in some predefined skill domain. This...can lead practitioners to neglect the complexity and multifaceted nature of learning.[5]

Liturgical formation is an example of a field that is complex, multifaceted, and not at all technological. In addition, some adults, including some students in theological schools, appear to show little desire to apply their learning to the liturgies they celebrate or to improve their liturgical celebrations. Therefore, a slightly different approach to learning is needed.

LEARNING THROUGH CRITICAL THINKING

A different approach to adult learning, often called **critical thinking**, seems to be more promising as a potentially effective method of liturgical formation. It has two main phases, (a) identifying and challenging assumptions, and (b) exploring and imagining alternatives. The first phase involves probing habitual ways of thinking and acting and examining their assumptions. For example, what is taken for granted regarding human nature and social institutions? What stereotypes are at work? Once these assumptions are identified, their accuracy and validity are evaluated. Are beliefs, values, and actions that have been taken for granted really suitable for our lives today? If not, they should be replaced. As well, in this first phase, the important effects of the cultural and historical context on assumptions, and on actions that arise from this context, come to be identified and appreciated. Established ways of thinking and acting reflect the culture and time in which we live, and our particular historical roots.

The second phase in critical thinking is to come to realize that alternatives exist to established ways of thinking and acting. Possibilities that extend beyond the empirically known universe of present ways of doing things need to be envisioned. Critical thinkers continually experiment with new ways of thinking about life and come to realize that many alternatives already exist in other cultural contexts. Of course, the assumptions behind such alternatives also need to be examined critically.

Relevant to the possible application of critical thinking to liturgical formation is the question whether it is compatible at all with commitment. On this point Brookfield states:

> As critical thinkers we can still hold passionately to certain beliefs, actions, and causes. However, our commitment is not slavish or uninformed, the result of successful socialization. Instead, it is arrived at after skeptical scrutiny and after being repeatedly tested against reality as we understand it; and this commitment is all the more strong because it has passed through the fire of this critical analysis. Our commitment is informed and rational, balanced by a recognition of its possible falsity.[6]

The exploration of assumptions and alternatives creates within the learners feelings of threat or disequilibrium. Chet Meyers points out:

Teachers should be acutely aware of the inher-
ently disruptive nature of this educative process.
Teaching critical thinking involves intentionally
creating an atmosphere of disequilibrium, so that
students can change, rework, or reconstruct their
thinking processes.

One reason that reconstructing thinking
processes can be painful is that structures of
thought are not merely matters of dispassionate
cognition. They are also highly personal and
emotional, involving cherished values and
beliefs.... Part of teaching critical thinking necessarily involves challenging students' implicit
theories and teaching them new perspectives for
interpretation. It can thus become a very
emotion-laden process.[7]

Meyers also points out that teachers need to provide "an
atmosphere of trust and support wherein students can let
go of some of the personal moorings that impose
limitations on the ways they think.... A teacher's enthusiasm, interest, and genuine concern help create a
challenging yet safe atmosphere in which students feel
confident enough to let go of old ways of thinking and try
out new ones."[8] Thus, as in other forms of adult education,
a variety of stimulating methods often are used to
enhance the motivation of students to learn.[9]

APPLICATION OF CRITICAL THINKING
TO LITURGICAL FORMATION

The critical thinking approach to adult learning has
been developed in secular circles and applied to non-
religious subject areas; it ignores any faith dimension of
human life. Yet many—though perhaps not all—aspects of
critical thinking theory seem compatible with Christian
faith. Indeed the movement from critical evaluation of life
assumptions to the exploration of alternatives seems very
much like the faith-journey of religious conversion and

spiritual growth. Critical thinking is concerned with transformation of lives, which is a central gospel value. It looks to an alternative future, for which the reign of God is a central biblical image.

Ways of Using Critical Thinking

How, in a general way, might critical thinking apply to liturgical formation? Critical thinkers see that their liturgical experiences, whether poor, mediocre or good, are and never will be perfect. Theologically, this is the recognition of human fallibility. Though liturgical perfection is a false and futile goal, continuing transformation is not. Critical thinkers ask what assumptions they themselves bring to liturgical celebrations, and ask to what extent they contribute to what is lacking in worship services. How much do they participate? To what extent do they really desire to participate? Is their participation at only the surface level of external actions? To what extent do they really appreciate and take ownership of the meaning of their participation? How, if at all, does their weekday living derive from and lead to Sunday worship? How is worship related to the whole of their spirituality? Critical thinkers also apply these and similar questions to other worshippers, to worship leaders, and to the local church community as a whole.

Critical thinking also can be applied to the order of service, choice of music and prayers, quality of ministry, the space in which worship is experienced, the pace of worship, opportunity for silence, and the relevance of preaching. This might be done differently in churches where worship is highly structured and in which official liturgical books are prescribed than in churches where there is greater opportunity for local composition and creativity. Nevertheless, even in the Roman Catholic Church it is a basic principle that "it is of the greatest importance that the celebration of the Mass...be so arranged that the ministers and the faithful...may more fully receive its good effects."[10] Likewise,

the pastoral effectiveness of a celebration will be
heightened if the texts of readings, prayers, and
songs correspond as closely as possible to the
needs, religious dispositions, and aptitude of the
participants. In planning the celebration, then,
the priest should consider the general spiritual
good of the assembly rather than his personal
outlook. He should be mindful that the choice of
texts is to be made in consultation with the
ministers and others who have a function in the
celebration, including the faithful.[11]

Critical thinkers question assumptions being made about
their own needs, religious disposition, and spiritual good,
and about those of their co-worshippers. Who makes
decisions regarding liturgical celebration, and upon what
information are these decisions made?

The importance of cultural expression in worship is
increasingly recognized by liturgists and churches, at least
in theory. It is acknowledged that, within limits, individual cultural groups should worship in ways that are
authentic to their cultures. Critical thinkers ask if this is
being done, what assumptions are made about cultural
expressions in worship, how authentic these expressions
are, and the extent to which they indeed are accepted and
interiorized by the worshippers. They also ask if such
principles of cultural adaptation do not apply to certain
subcultures as children, teenagers, women, persons with
disabilities, and older persons, then why is more not done
to promote the full participation in worship of these
members of local church communities.

Critical thinkers ask why the contemporary liturgical
movement is not being carried forward in many
churches. Some churches seem to have stopped with the
recovery of the best practices of the past and the
elimination of less desirable or beneficial practices. They
seem reluctant to take the next step, which is the visioning

of alternatives that are most suitable for the 21st century. Why is this? What assumptions are being made?

The second phase of critical thinking is to explore and imagine alternatives. Some worshippers and worship leaders seem quite content with worship as it now is, even if mediocre or poor according to one or another criteria. Why do they not desire something better, more inclusive and life-giving? What assumptions are involved in this phenomenon?

What are the visions of those who do seek change? How might these be put into practice, either with the present liturgy of their church, or with changes in texts, music, or orders of service? How can visioning an alternative future in worship go beyond the surface—what we do—and penetrate to the dimensions of meaning, daily living, ministry and witness, and spirituality?

Both phases of critical thinking can be applied not only to the worship service itself, but also to its consequences in the daily living of worshippers. If people do not appreciate how their liturgical experiences relate to social issues such as unemployment, immigration, land claims, and poverty, for example, then there is a need to improve both their liturgies and their liturgical formation. Much has already been written on this subject.[12]

Teaching Liturgy Critically

How might these general applications of critical thinking to liturgical formation be organized in a course on liturgy? Surely this might be accomplished in a variety of ways, and there is a great need to explore diverse possibilities in this regard. At the present time there is simply very little experience. However, a course on worship and homiletics which Denise Davis Taylor and I gave in 1993, endeavored to embody at least some principles of critical thinking and provided at least some experience in this approach to teaching and learning. This course is described briefly here.

Most of the approximately thirty participants were

candidates for diaconal ministry in the United Church of Canada; a few others were studying for their Master's degree or Certificate in Theological Studies. All but two participants were women, and most were members of the United Church; others came from the Presbyterian and Unitarian churches. Several of the United Church members had grown up in the Anglican or Roman Catholic churches. Because participants live throughout central and western Canada, they come together only occasionally for concentrated residential courses; this one was for five consecutive days—thirty-five hours. They were accustomed to studying in pairs and small groups.

The central theme of the course was the liturgical experience of the participants before, during, and after the five days. Some time before the formal beginning of the course, participants started to keep a journal related to their Sunday worship experiences. They noted what they did, reported their feelings and reflections, and identified questions that arose in their minds. They were asked to focus and name their questions and issues related to worship and bring them to the course.

Critical reflection was initiated by also asking participants to read and reflect on two books before the formal beginning of the course. James White's *Protestant Worship*[13] helped participants to recognize the assumptions of their worship experiences from an historical perspective. In addition, by comparing the worship traditions of a number of church traditions in parallel chapters, participants were introduced to alternative visions of worship. The second book, Marjorie Procter-Smith's *In Her Own Rite*,[14] presents a critique of many assumptions regarding worship from the perspective of feminist theology.

Through liturgical celebration it is possible to provide actual experiences of alternative visions of worship. Thus at the beginning of each of the first three days of the course, all participants engaged in liturgies that were obviously related to what they did at home, but were also clearly different. These were a gathering liturgy, a liturgy of the word, and a table liturgy; all had been planned ahead of time by the facilitators. On the fourth day, which was a Sunday, participants were asked to plan and lead "the kind of Sunday service they had always dreamed about"; three hours were given to planning and celebrating this liturgy. They were to use their own past experiences, their learnings so far in the course, and their own creativity. On the fifth day all celebrated a type of liturgy that was new to everyone (though planned by the facilitators): a liturgy of lament for sexual abuse and domestic violence. Each day also ended with brief liturgies of kinds most participants had not previously experienced.

Finally, after they returned home, participants were asked to prepare a worship service for their own congregation (or another local group) that would provide some alternative experiences while respecting the limits imposed by local custom and needs. They were to decide on the order of service, compose prayers and sermon, choose music, and decide how ministry would be shared and carried out. In addition, they were to provide a detailed rationale for their choices, as well as an assessment of the response of the congregation.

Following each day's opening liturgy, the questioning of assumptions and imagining of alternatives was applied to specific aspects of worship services: the basic patterns of worship, nonverbal elements (space, time, embodiment, symbol, and symbolic action), verbal elements (narrative and poetic language, inclusive language, scripture, preaching, various kinds of prayers, and other liturgical texts), and musical elements. Woven across these strands were the question of meaning (how was God named? ourselves? the church?) and the question of the connections between worship and daily living.

A wide variety of methods were used to do all this. For example, the actual experience of being asked to write short prayers for liturgical use raised many questions.

What is prayer? What is the rationale for a prayer of petition? Who is the God to whom the prayers are addressed? Suggested guidelines for inclusive language also generated much discussion. In both cases some discomfort was generated among the participants. This was eased by patience and caring on the part of the facilitators, as well as mutual support—and challenge—from other participants.

Space precludes description of other parts of the course. In general, participants appreciated the role given to liturgical experience and the extensive use of liturgies that provided alternatives to what they were used to. Many participants were already familiar with a critical approach to theology, and were critical as well of aspects of their regular liturgies at home. Providing basic principles of the church's heritage as well as alternative ways of expressing these liturgically was well received. Of course, there was not enough time to do everything that might be desired! Having five full days all together had both advantages and disadvantages. There was a continuity and unity to the course; there was also little or no time for reflection, reading, and additional planning between classes.

This approach could easily be applied to weekly sessions of two or three hours in local church communities. The initial liturgy would be brief, and much of the reflection would be based on the Sunday worship experiences of the participants. Thinking critically about the Sunday liturgy and on its effects in their lives will lead to envisioning alternatives that are more satisfying and more challenging.

Challenges to the Use of Critical Thinking

Potential obstacles that might prevent the use of critical thinking in liturgical formation are similar to those that affect other approaches to adult learning.[15] Teachers may be untrained in this mode of education. They may be unaware of adult education approaches in general, or of critical thinking in particular. If aware, they may not be sympathetic or interested. If committed to this approach, they may not have the experience or skills to carry it out. Learners, too, may not be ready to engage in critical thinking, and may need persuasion, preparation, and encouragement.

Institutional factors may impede use of critical thinking as well. Curriculum constraints, class schedules, grading policies, and resources available may present difficulties. In addition, the attitudes of administrators and other faculty members toward adult learning and critical thinking may constitute negative influences. Finally, the critical thinking approach is time consuming and involves closer contact with learners than may be desired by teachers and administrators.

Though full-day classes are not essential, it is clear that two and preferably three hour segments are essential for including both liturgical experiences, satisfactory reflection and responses to these, and critical thinking about assumptions and the constitutive elements of liturgical celebration. Fifty-minute classes are completely inadequate.[16]

Critical thinking represents only one approach to liturgical formation, and one that needs further trial and experimentation. It appears to have the potential for including in a serious way the affective and spiritual dimensions of liturgical experience. It also has the potential for being able to take learners on a journey of conversion and transformation with respect to the full, active and conscious participation that is their right and which other educational approaches seem unable to accomplish.

DISCUSSION QUESTIONS

1. In what ways do you participate in your own Sunday liturgy? Do you feel that you participate fully, actively and consciously? In what ways do you feel that your participation might be improved?

2. In what ways does your Sunday worship affect how you live during the week? Do you think you need to learn more about the connections between liturgy and daily living? Have these connections ever been discussed in your community? How, and to what effect?

3. Does thinking critically about your Sunday worship and envisioning alternatives to present practices excite you, threaten you, or both?

4. Can you think of ways of applying critical thinking for the purpose of liturgical formation in your own setting? What group would you work with, and how would you get started?

NOTES

1. Constitution on the Liturgy, n.14. *Documents on the Liturgy 1963-1979. Consiliar, Papal, and Curial Texts.* International Commission on English in the Liturgy (Collegeville, MN.: Liturgical Press, 1982), p. 8.

2. See, for example, Stephen D. Brookfield, *Understanding and Facilitating Adult Learning* (San Francisco: Jossey-Bass, 1986); Stephen D. Brookfield, *Developing Critical Thinkers: Challenging Adults to Explore Alternative Ways of Thinking and Acting* (San Francisco: Jossey-Bass, 1987); Jack Mezirow and Associates, *Fostering Critical Reflection in Adulthood: A Guide to Transformative and Emancipatory Learning* (San Francisco: Jossey-Bass, 1991).

3. A summary of critiques of andragogy is found in Brookfield, *Understanding and Facilitating Adult Learning*, chapter 5.

4. Ibid., p. 98

5. Ibid., p. 99

6. Brookfield, *Developing Critical Thinkers*, p. 23.

7. Meyers, *Teaching Students to Think Critically*, p. 14.

8. Ibid., p. 99.

9. See, for example, Mezirow and Associates, *Fostering Critical Reflection in Adulthood*; Meyers, *Teaching Students to Think Critically*; and Raymond J. Wlodkowski, *Enhancing Adult Motivation to Learn* (San Francisco: Jossey-Bass, 1991).

10. General Instruction of the Roman Missal, no.2

11. Ibid., no. 313.

12. See, for example, J. Frank Henderson, "Liturgy and the Faith-Formation of Adults: The Distance Between Vision and Practice," *Insight: A Resource for Adult Religious Education* (1991), pp. 40-49; J. Frank Henderson, Stephen Larson, and Kathleen Quinn, *Liturgy, Justice and the Reign of God: Vision and Practice* (New York: Paulist Press, 1989); J. Frank Henderson, "Liturgy, Justice, and Daily Life," *National Bulletin on Liturgy* 26, no. 136 (Winter, 1993), pp. 224-232.

13. James White, *Protestant Worship: Traditions in Transition* (Louisville, Ky.: Westminster/John Knox Press, 1989).

14. Marjorie Procter-Smith, *In Her Own Rite: Constructing Feminist Liturgical Tradition* (Nashville, Tenn.: Abingdon, 1990).

15. See Brookfield, *Understanding and Facilitating Adult Learning*, pp. 68-69.

16. On this point see also Meyers, *Teaching Students to Think Critically*, pp. 37, 42-43.

ABOUT THE AUTHOR

J. Frank Henderson is former professor of bio-chemistry and cancer research at the University of Alberta as well as adjunct professor in liturgy at Newman Theological College, St. Stephen's College, and St. Paul University; he also teaches preaching and ecumenism. He is editor of the *National Bulletin on Liturgy*, published by the Canadian Conference of Catholic Bishops. With

Stephen Larson and Kathleen Quinn he is coauthor of *Liturgy, Justice and the Reign of God: Vision and Practice* (1989); with Mary Schaefer he wrote *The Catholic Priesthood: A Liturgically Based Theology of the Presbyteral Office* (1990). He lives in Edmonton, Alberta, with his wife Ruth.

3. LISTENING TO THE VOICES OF THE PEOPLE:

A CASE STUDY OF CULTURAL FACTORS IN NATIVE COMMUNITIES

J. Gregory Dunwoody

Adult religious education takes place within a cultural context. The content, the methods, even the language of adult religious education are all influenced by culture. The influence is even greater in a cross-cultural experience of adult religious education. Both culture and religion are community-based. That is, the meanings and values conveyed by culture and religion come from the community. Our efforts in adult religious education must take into consideration the cultural factors of any particular community.

This chapter offers some reflective ideas and experiences on adult religious education among Native people, especially the Ojibway and Cree peoples. These ideas may stimulate further ideas that are applicable to other cultural communities—for example, Afro-Americans/Canadians, Hispanics, Vietnamese, Koreans, Ukrainians, and so forth. An important point in this chapter is to listen to the voices of the people within any cultural community, and to build adult religious educational programs around the ideas and suggestions coming forth through these cultural voices.

Native people are providing a very vibrant spiritual leadership in the life of their communities. Some of this new leadership has come about because the churches have a newly found respect for traditional Native culture and spirituality. Also, some of this has come about because of new attitudes and approaches in adult religious education. However, much of this has come about because the power of the Creator ought not to have been suppressed, and can no longer be suppressed, by the dominant society and—in some cases—by the churches.

This chapter describes four key cultural orientations which Native people bring to their religious educational perceptions today. These are traditional culture and spirituality, Kitchi-Manitou and creation, the sacred circle, and holistic healing. Some practical considerations for adult religious education are given after each orientation. The chapter concludes by identifying key approaches for adult religious education whenever cultural factors are important.

I wish to note that I am not speaking for Native people. They can and do speak eloquently in their own right about their own spiritualities, values, and customs. This I wish to respect. In this chapter I hope to share what I, as a non-Native, have heard, seen, and learned in doing adult religious education in the Native context. These learnings come out of my contacts mostly with the Ojibway and Cree peoples. There are various Native peoples, and thus various Native cultures and spiritualities across North America. They may share some common elements. However, the reflective ideas which follow are based on what I have heard and learned from the Ojibway and Cree peoples.

CONSEQUENCES OF THE DOCTRINE OF DISCOVERY

Cultural considerations that relate to adult religious education among Native people must begin by noting the consequences which 500 years of conquest has had for them. Although Native people have much to celebrate, they have much to struggle with. These struggles provide the context and environment within which adult religious education takes place.

Native people have survived 500 years of conquest with disastrous consequences. The "doctrine of discovery," as Harold Cardinal calls this conquest,[1] led European nations to believe that they had the God-given right to claim lands and peoples. As a consequence of 500 years of oppression, Native people today have lost much of their cultural and spiritual identities. They have lost much of their traditional way of life. The end results have been disastrous. Many Native communities have extremely high rates of addictions, abuse (physical, sexual, emotional), family breakdown, and unemployment.

> We recognize that many of the problems that beset native communities today—high unemployment, alcoholism, family breakdown, domestic violence, spiralling suicide rates, lack of healthy self-esteem—are not so much the result of personal failure as they are the result of centuries of systemic imperialism.[2]
>
> *Douglas Crosby, O.M.I., President, Oblate Conference of Canada, to over 15,000 Native people at Lac St. Anne., Alberta*

It is important to remember that Native people had a full system of education, medical care, government, employment, and spirituality before the European conquest! These were either destroyed or seriously imperiled by the European and missionary conquest.

In many Native communities unemployment is often as high as eighty percent.[3] Church leadership have called an eleven percent unemployment rate in the general society "a moral disorder, a social evil."[4] One wonders what they would say about an 80 percent unemployment rate. For Native men the average age at death is twenty-five years younger than non-Native men. For Native women, it is twenty-eight years younger. Infant mortality rates are higher than the national average. The suicide rate is more than double the non-Native rate. In some parts of North America less than fifty percent of Native homes have indoor plumbing. The self-esteem, the self-image, the self-confidence, and the community threads of

Native people have been badly shaken or shattered. These statistics and facts are real life issues and thus important to adult religious educators.

In recent times the churches are becoming more aware of their own participation in the doctrine of discovery. Native religious practices, in Canada for example, were prohibited since 1884 by amendments to the Indian Act.[5] Legislation in 1890 in the United States limited the religious freedom for Native people and made participation in many religious ceremonies a crime.[6] For generations Native people were prohibited and punished for practising their spiritual traditions. Only in 1951 was the Indian Act (Canada) amended to permit Native people freedom of religious expression. During the long period of religious prohibition the churches often supported government practices. They did this, for instance, by running residential schools which supported the goal of assimilation of Native people into the dominant society. Native children were taken away from their families; from their communal and traditional way of living. Frequently they were punished for speaking their own language. Government supported, church run, residential schools have been closed for a couple of decades now. Yet it is only in recent times that practices of physical, emotional, and sexual abuse in the schools are surfacing.

Church leaders are beginning to recognize, and take responsibility for, the destructive role which churches have played over the years. Douglas Crosby, president of the Oblate Conference of Canada recently said, "We apologize for the part we played in the cultural, ethnic, linguistic, and religious imperialism that was part of the mentality with which the peoples of Europe first met the aboriginal peoples and which consistently has lurked behind the way the Native peoples of Canada have been treated by civil government and by the Churches."[7] Robert Smith, the Moderator of the United Church of Canada, also offered an apology as part of a reconciliation process between the United Church and Native people. Part of what he said was: "Long before my people journeyed to this land...you received from your elders an understanding of creation and of the mystery that surrounds us all...we did not hear you when you shared your vision."[8] Today, in most instances, the churches and Native people are working on healing and reconciliation.

The adult religious educator must be aware that the Creator, the Mystery we call God, has already spoken to the Native people. They have heard the Creator and already have their own ways and understandings of the Creator.

The adult religious educator must also be aware that the Native people realize that some of what the churches brought in the past was harmful, and that it was often imposed. The religious educators' approach for this reason must be very humble and extremely attentive. Their primary attitude within a church context must be one of listening. The churches today need to walk quietly alongside Native people. Adult religious education must support how Native people themselves hear and respond to the Creator. The content of adult religious education must address the lost or suppressed spiritual and cultural needs of Native people, as Native people themselves identify them.

Any education among adults must be very practical and address the real and immediate life issues. The religious content and character of adult religious education must be grounded in a God who relates to the people of God in the here and now. Native people, both in life and in language, are very practical.

The wider field of adult education has, for a long time, espoused the principle that effective adult education is problem-centered or practical and that it should be of immediate use or value to the adult. David Boud tells us that problem-based learning is older than formal education itself. The principle idea on which it is based is "that the starting point for the learning should be a problem, a query such as a puzzle that the learner wishes to solve."[9] Problem-based learning acknowledges that learners make an important contribution to learning by drawing upon their own experience. Thus, it is grounded in the practical. This type of learning is very suitable for Native people.

The cultural context is another dimension of learning that relates to the practical and that colors the needs and values of the adult learner. Peter Hart in writing about the Dene people of the Northwest Territories talks about cultural relevance in terms of practices. He notes, for example, the use of the circle for meetings rather than arranged rows. For the Dene, "the circle represents an integrated and whole reality—four winds, four directions, four seasons."[10] The arrangement in rows makes no natural sense to the Dene; it is neither practical nor useful.

In the remainder of this chapter I describe how I have experienced the four key orientations that Native people emphasize in their life today. These are: reclaiming traditional culture and spirituality, respecting Kitchi-Manitou and creation, living the sacred circle, and seeking holistic healing. For each of these orientations some practical considerations for adult religious education are given.

RECLAIMING TRADITIONAL CULTURE AND SPIRITUALITY

> The philosophy of the original people was based on the timelessness and the harmony and the power of the Creation, and humanity's place and purpose in it. And because of the fundamental difference we could not, and we never can "be like him." God never intended for roses to become daisies.[11]
>
> *Arthur Solomon, Anishnawbe spiritual teacher*

Native people are reclaiming their traditional cultural and spiritual ways. The last few decades especially have seen some dramatic changes in the lives of

Native people. They have claimed self-government, or ownership, in many areas where non-Natives had had control. Native people are increasingly governing their own child and family service organizations, educational systems, justice systems, business and economic development, and community government.

This self-government means that Native people themselves can meet, decide, and carry out their daily life activities in ways that are faithful to their own cultural and spiritual ways. As Native people take responsibility to live according to their values, there is a restoration of pride and dignity. The reclaiming of traditional culture and spirituality raises important considerations for adult religious education.

Considerations of Self-Determination

A first consideration is that Native people must be given self-government in their own churches, ministry training, and adult religious education. Most religious denominations officially support Native people when they ask for self-government from society at large. Yet, there is a reluctance, often unconscious, to offer Native people self-government within the church. For example, ministry training and ministry recognition often follows the pattern and methods used for non-Native people. Some Native spirituality may be incorporated into the pattern, but the dominant non-Native approach still remains. In some cases a Native approach to ministry training is taken, but it creates a second-class ministry or leadership in the church. As one Native deacon told me, "Now that we are trained and ordained we are left sitting quietly like cans of soup on a store shelf." In adult religious education Native people must have self-government over the educating-learning process.

One denomination in which I believe the Native people have a fair degree of self-government within their own denomination is in the United Church of Canada. They have established the Dr. Jessie Saulteaux Resource

Centre[12] for ministry and theological training for leadership development, and for cross-cultural understanding. Here the methods of training and the content are strongly faithful to Native cultural and spiritual ways. The United Church of Canada has also established the All-Native Circle Conference[13] so that the administration and support of Native churches can also be faithful to Native tradition.

A second consideration is that the churches, and adult religious education, must accept "inculturation" of the gospel. By inculturation I mean the right of another people to hear and to respond to the Good News of Jesus in faithfulness to their own cultural and spiritual traditions.[14] While the Good News transcends every culture, it takes root in and is always expressed through culture! Through inculturation wholly new expressions of living out the gospel will be born. Openness to inculturation must be part of the adult religious education process, ministry training, or community action. When the adult religious educator is non-Native, it is especially important to catch oneself and suspend judgment when new values and responses are being undertaken. We must really listen as we walk along another's cultural and spiritual path.

Care in Choice of Words

The right to cultural expression and self-government in a truly Native church raises a very critical question: would it be acceptable to support the development of an autonomous Native Christian church even if it might no longer belong to our denomination? That is, are the denominational churches really open to having a wholly new expression of Christianity being born? In many cultural situations, adult religious educators reflect the values of and are even supported by the sponsoring institution or denomination. In cross-cultural adult religious education, who really retains ownership over the goals and decision-making?

An important cross-cultural consideration for adult religious education is attentiveness to the words we use. A word brings a whole sense of meaning and feeling which has been constructed socially and culturally. One cannot assume in any situation, but even more so in a cross-cultural situation, that a word means the same thing to all people. I often slow down the process, especially if key words, images, or symbols are being used. It's good to ask people about the meaning and original understanding behind a word. For example, if I as a non-Native wish to use the word "chief" it may be because it means something to me about leadership or responsibility. Yet, all the time I am using the word "chief" the Native people are hearing and feeling the word differently. For example, the Ojibway word for chief is "ogimaakaan," "ogimaa," meaning someone who is rich, wealthy, or has money, although rich and wealthy are understood as more than simply money. Ogimaa comes from the word which they have for the government which means the greatest wealthy person. Yet added to the word "ogimaa" is "kaan" which means "pretending to be." So, while a chief is understood as the chief or leader in practice, the understanding is also that he is pretending to be rich, pretending to be the boss. Indeed, in some cases the structure of choosing a chief was imposed by the government. George Tinker conveys the challenge and the difficulties behind different languages and words, especially in the religious context. He writes, "the categories of discourse simply do not translate from one language or culture to another as if they were mere codes for one another that need only be transcribed."[15] George Tinker mentions that even the notion of "God" was unknown to Native peoples and the European meaning had to be filled in.

Considerations of Ritual

Another consideration for adult religious education arises as Native people reclaim their spiritual tradition: ritual or worship must become part of the educational process. Ritual plays an important part in Native spiritual learning. Liturgy and learning are very much connected. Adult religious education needs to give higher importance to the place of ritual and symbol in the educational process. Much of the current practice of adult religious education reflects the general educational practice in a society where education and religion are separated. However, the spiritual part of human beings cannot be separated from the emotional, physical, or intellectual. Good education addresses the spirit of the person, and worship or ritual is a very effective method of spiritual learning and insight.

When incorporating Native rituals and symbols I offer a caution. The value of Native rituals and symbols is sometimes trivialized when double-ritualizing takes place. Double-ritualizing is when a traditional cultural ritual is immediately followed by a non-Native ritual. It is as if the dominant culture's ritual is the only spiritual one that works! It is important that non-Native people are supportive of those Native people who wish to accept Native ways of expressing their faith.

RESPECTING KITCHI-MANITOU AND CREATION

We were sitting in a circle. She took the small stone into her hand. To all appearances the stone was rather insignificant. She held it in silence for a long time. Then tears came flowing down her cheeks. Her hand was shaking, and she started to speak in a trembling voice. Creation had touched her. She was sharing her truth.[16]

Creation is a vital part of the Native way of life. Creation speaks to the Native people. They listen, and then they speak what they have heard. Kitchi-Manitou, "the Great Mystery,"[17] had a vision or dream and brought that dream, creation, into existence. There are plants and animals, two and four legged, birds and fish, and all have special powers. Basil Johnston, a Native teacher, says that

Native people know that all human beings are "last in the order of creation, least in the order of dependence, and weakest in bodily powers,"[18] and we are "co-tenants on the earth." [19] In spite of this, human beings have the greatest gift: the ability to dream. So, human beings share in creation and in creating. From creation human beings learn balance and harmony. Everything has its place and time.

The respect for creation is shown in how Native people live on earth. The land, commonly called "mother earth," belongs to the Creator. It can never be owned. Mother earth gave birth to us and sustains us. The great respect Native people have for the land and all living things is shown, for example, when they offer tobacco back to mother earth in thanksgiving for anything they have taken. Whether taken for food or medicine or rituals, it is important to show thanks to mother earth for the gift she gives.

I remember one time when a presentation of cut flowers was given to a particular lady. One of the elders quietly asked me, "Why did they give her cut flowers?" Because the answer seemed rather obvious to me, I repeated his question back to him. He said, "Why did they 'cut' flowers that were alive? Native people would not do this." All things in creation are living and each has its place, its balance in life. Being aware of that balance in life teaches great lessons in spiritual living.

Listening to Creation

To touch and to listen to creation is an important consideration for adult religious education. The strong link to creation that Native people feel must be respected. It's preferable, then, that spiritual learning take place out on mother earth. The setting for adult religious education should be connected to the land. We often hold our learning sessions outside in the open. This way we can be very close to creation and the Creator. Another choice might be to meet at retreat or ministry training centers which are located in natural settings.

With the increasing numbers of Native people migrating to the major cities it is important that adult religious education efforts be connected to nature, to the land. Sometimes Native people have lived in the city for two or three generations. When given a chance to meet outside the city, closer to nature, they really become more alive and hopeful. When Native people do meet in the city, as the circle I work with does, items from nature are in plain and immediate view. These may be rocks, plants, earth, or water. They are usually placed in the middle of our circle. They remind Native people of what is most natural and good in creation and in themselves.

Symbols of creation speak to us more powerfully than words. Symbols from nature are an important part of restoring ritual or worship to the religious education process. In the beginning most symbols of mainstream religions were probably very natural, but sacred all the same! Over time the traditional Christian symbols, for example, have become so removed from the people, have become so small and so sacred, that we can't touch them any longer; consequently they are now lost to large numbers of people. I think here of the small communion wafer which is supposed to be the bread of life. Or, the tiny dab of oil which is supposed to signify healing. Those Christian movements, and I refer here to the Charismatic movement, which have large and distinct symbols which people can touch and be touched by may have appeal for Native people.

Another important point is that creation is the starting point for adult religious education. Religious education among Native people starts from observing and participating in all of creation. This includes observing and sharing about one's self. Storytelling is an excellent method for learning about creation. Native people often gather to tell stories about creation and about themselves. They learn truth and righteous ways of living from these.

Formerly, religious education seemed to start either with Jesus or with dogmatic teaching. The first act of the Creator was not explanation. It was creation!

Assuming a Humble Role

Knowing the place of human beings in creation leads to another important consideration: each human being, especially the adult religious educator, must be humble! Native speakers, especially the most respected elders, begin by stating their own smallness before the Creator and all of creation. They regularly ask for forgiveness for any past hurts they may have caused. They ask, too, for forgiveness for any hurt they may cause, however unintentional, by what they are about to say. A carrier of the sacred pipe, for example, cannot carry or pray with the pipe unless he or she carries no grudges, uses no addictive substances, and forgives others. Indeed, the pipe carrier carries the sacred pipe for the community. In the Christian context, one does not offer a gift at the altar without first being reconciled with one's brother (Matthew 5:24). The traditional Native speaker concludes in humility. Thanks is offered to the Creator for all the blessings received. Thanks is also given to those who have listened. The facilitator of adult religious education must strive for this same humility in both words, actions, and even the use of sacred symbols or objects (for example, the Bible).

Each day Native gatherings begin with a humble ritual of cleansing. This is done, for example, through smudging oneself with the smoke of the sweetgrass. As the day begins each person cleanses himself or herself in the sacred smudge. It is important to remember our smallness before the Creator. This sweetgrass ceremony is often used to begin our learning sessions.

Lastly, respect for creation also determines the kind of language to be used. The language must be practical, earthy, and clear. Education leads to practical living. The language of adult religious education should not be too conceptual or theoretical. The Creator is more interested in application than explanation.

LIVING THE SACRED CIRCLE

> He asked if he could say a few words before the worship ended. He wanted to share that he was so happy to be meeting in the church and sitting in a circle. It was good, he was saying, to sit as equals, to have the priest sitting in the circle; to be able to see and pray with one another face to face. He never thought that praying in a circle, the Native way, would come so soon in his church.[20]

The harmony and the balance of creation is taught and respected through the sacred cycle. Sometimes called the medicine wheel or the healing wheel, the sacred circle teaches much about the sacred cycle of creation. In creation the sun rises in the east each day and circles over and around us. Even when the sun goes down in the west, Native people know that it will pass under us and rise again in the east. Native people want to respect this cycle, this harmony or balance, in creation.

The sacred circle unites the four directions. Each direction has one of the four colors—red, yellow, black, and white—to teach, among other things, that all peoples have a special place and are called to live in harmony. Each direction around the circle also teaches that there is a place for youth, for women, for elders, and for ancestors. Each direction teaches humans to respect one of the four sacred elements of creation: earth, air, water, and fire. The sacred cycle also teaches us to include all four parts of human nature: the physical, emotional, intellectual, and spiritual. All are equally important and related to one another.[21]

The sacred circle teaches equality and inclusiveness. It teaches that all belong. Children, for example, are always welcomed to Native gatherings. Even as a child, one learns spiritual ways to the degree that one is ready to listen to and observe the path which others follow. Women also have very important roles. In fact, some sacred rituals can only be done by women. Elders are also included in Native gatherings. Frequently theirs is the first word spoken. Meetings will not start without the elders being present. Projects will not be undertaken without the blessing of the elders.

Respect for the Circle

Adult religious education sessions among Native people need to respect the sacred circle. This can be done by meeting in a circle where all, educators and learners, are seen as equals. In a circle there is no beginning and no end. All belong equally. When the sharing takes place in the circle we go to the left, sometimes beginning in the east, because this is the direction in which the sacred circle of creation moves each day. I was told by a Native elder that I worried too much about leadership training. Her explanation was that when the circle needs a leader one would be chosen, otherwise the circle is not ready for a leader.

Generally, in the dominant society, we do not respect the circle of creation. We tend to organize and control people by placing them in rows. Consider four social institutions: the churches, courts, schools, and policing. All four institutions have tended to meet or operate in rows. This separates those in power, who often occupy a different or sacred space, from others. All four of these institutions have not been very effective or healthy historically for Native people. Ironically, many of us in the wider society are also wondering just how effective and healthy these institutions have been for us. It is important for all human beings to live as equals.

The equality experienced in the sacred circle challenges those adult religious education approaches that tend to be hierarchical and dogmatic, even legalistic. Spiritual learning among Native people is enhanced when the power of the sacred circle is respected. This is done by all sharing their own voice as to how they hear the Creator speaking. One voice ought not to speak louder than others. The crane is a symbol of leadership because its voice is seldom heard, and it speaks only when all others are silently listening.[22]

Dogmatic or legalistic content and approaches to adult religious education do not work among Native people. Observing nature's way, "the ethic of non-interference" promotes "positive interpersonal relationships by discouraging coercion of any kind, be it physical, verbal, or psychological."[23] Each part of creation learns to live in harmony with the others through listening and observing. If not, creation itself will eventually discipline or teach the lesson. Getting wet in the cold of winter, for example, is punishment enough from creation. One does not need others to tell you what is right or wrong. If others have to tell me what I am not ready to hear, or to coerce me, then I am not ready to learn. This applies to the spiritual way. It is important that each one in the sacred circle listens in order to seek the truth together. It is more important to first listen and observe than it is to speak or interfere.

Concern for the Community

A second consideration the sacred circle brings to adult religious education is concern for the community. Much of mainstream adult education has tended to emphasize individual growth and individual learning. This emphasis continues even if we do happen to meet in groups. Native people believe strongly that individual living is best achieved when it takes place within family and community living.

I remember one time when a Native person spoke passionately about his ideas as to what should be done about a certain issue that concerned everyone. From previous private conversations I also knew that others disagreed with what was being proposed. Yet no one said anything. The individual was left free to do as he wished. I visited an elder that evening and asked him why no one had objected. His response was that Native people want to respect people when they are out in public. He added that Native people also know that any individual will need, sooner or later, the community. Individuals, even when they go off by themselves, will come back to the community. This trust in the community process and the community coming to a decision on its own time is a very strong challenge for adult religious education. In the religious context, especially, our efforts need to be open to doing things in God's time.

Methods of adult religious education should be chosen to reflect Natives' emphasis on community. In one ministry training project I introduced the notion of "individual learning covenants."[24] As participants evaluated this approach they were quite clear in asking also for "community" covenants. While they wanted some individual learning, they wanted to know how they could learn more as a community. "Community models of learning"[25] are very important in the Native context. Some Native people find themselves in very oppressed situations. The Highlander approach[26] to community learning can be very helpful. At their Folk Schools adult learning takes place within the context of community action initiatives. Adult religious education needs to respect the importance and the primacy of the learning community.

Symbols in adult religious education should be used with special caution especially symbols from another culture. It is very important that the adult educator listen, and listen again, to the meaning of any symbol. The real meaning or power of the symbol comes from the people themselves, their own cultural context. So, adult religious educators must avoid the attitude of only listening long enough to be able to "use" the symbol to convey the educator's agenda or message. If symbols from another culture are only "used," as if there is some new-found fascination (as sometimes occurs in the New Age movement), then we both deprive people of the dignity of owning their own culture and deprive ourselves of the real challenges and learnings which can come from the symbol. I think here of the sacred wheel and all the teachings it contains relating to the number "four." If I, as a Christian, simply use the symbol to illustrate my Christian teachings, then I may fail to see the challenges it contains to the Christian way of believing. For example, one challenge it presents is that completeness and wholeness comes in "fours." This fact begs the question, how can God then be limited to only three persons in the one mystery we have named God?

SEEKING HOLISTIC HEALING

When I encounter angry people, I remember my own anger and I know theirs comes from some pain. Most of us had to go on a personal healing journey.[27]

Native Social Worker as reported
by Dorothy Lachance

These words by a Native outreach worker and counsellor illustrate how healing is a very important part of the Native way of life today. As each of us walks our journey on mother earth we become aware of our own need for healing. As we walk upon the path we can listen to the emotional, physical, mental, and spiritual parts of our lives. If we listen, then we become keenly aware that we are in need of healing. We observe the environment and see that mother earth is in need of healing. We observe the people on mother earth and we see that all peoples are in need of healing. Many Native communities have "Healing Circles." Calling the people together to solve a problem is a key to community life. So, Native people call the sacred circle together in order to seek holistic healing.

Concept of Holistic Healing

Native people have not found the outside ways of healing to be too successful. The dominant non-Native society often seeks healing in highly individualistic and professional ways. The attitude of the dominant society is easily seen in such catchy excuses as: "Who am I to interfere?" "What can one person do?" "If no one else is being hurt, then let it go." This keeps everything private and so we avoid dealing with the pain of others. We avoid both accountability to the community and the community's support for our healing. Sometimes the non-Native society seeks a consumer approach of quick fixes, be they medical, psychological, or even spiritual. The non-Native society even proposes that people should be incarcerated and sent away to jails. Does punishment really lead to healing? If so, then North America, with its highest incarceration rate, should be the safest and most healing place to live in the world. Non-Native approaches often place people outside of their community and these are very inefficient ways to bring about healing. They are destructive of both individuals and the community. Punishing people through jails only increases the violence, builds more jails, and fails to restore harmony to the community.

One Native project of healing is the "Community Holistic Healing Center" in Hollow Water.[28] The people of Hollow Water use the whole community to help victims, abusers, and their families. The circle of healing operates on the principles that the community must be involved and that neither victim nor community can grow toward wholeness until the victimizer is healed. The heart of the circle of healing is the opportunity for community members to speak. They tell the abuser how they feel about what has happened, be the abuse physical, emotional, sexual, or an addiction. People share how they have been affected, and they offer their support to both victim and victimizer.

The Native way of healing is to work always toward

forgiveness. Native people want to restore the balance in relationships. They do not want to punish or banish people. The healing process between the circle of healing and the individual takes time. Healing and forgiveness do not come quickly or easily, but they are sought after.

Application of Holistic Healing Concepts in Adult Religious Education

The focus of adult religious education must be on the very practical and real needs people have for healing. Ironically, perhaps, we grow spiritually out of our own woundedness—out of our own need for healing. Participation in the circle of healing invites one to be honest about one's own need for healing. It invites one, again, to be humble in just how one's own spiritual life falls short of holistic living.

Another consideration is that the adult religious educator's efforts must be connected to the efforts of others. Hollow Water's approach to the circle of healing has participation from church staff as well as key church members. In many communities child and family workers, addiction counsellors, welfare and social service people, all work in painful situations needing healing and support. The church cannot work in isolation from, or without connection to these people. If the church educates on its own agenda, then it leaves Christian spirituality open to the accusation that it has nothing to do with the daily lives and needs of the people.

If adult religious education does bring any message, it must be seen as "Good News" offering practical hope. Adult religious education should be undertaken as hope-filled collaboration in the practical projects which Native people themselves have chosen. Rather than leading people to a sense of depression and powerlessness, which some religious approaches do, adult religious education must enable people to feel alive and to live with dignity and hope. Too much religious education has been intellectual and conceptual (a nauseating discussion of ideas) without any practical and life-giving building of self-esteem, relationships, or community.

The human need for healing reminds us that adult religious education is a very human effort. It is in our humanity that we discover our spiritual hunger and way. Those of us in the Christian tradition ought to speak more about the humanity of Jesus. Perhaps we have over-emphasized the divinity of Jesus. Perhaps we have tended to see Jesus as God out there or up there. Jesus is not a rather distant figure who identifies little with what we live each day in our woundedness, in our humanness. Jesus was, and still is, God among us as one of us.

USEFULNESS OF THIS CASE STUDY FOR WIDER PERSPECTIVES OF CULTURAL FACTORS

I have outlined a path of adult religious education which I have experienced among Native peoples. My aim has been to illustrate the importance of listening to cultural factors in any adult religious educational effort. I have done this by describing those practical considerations in adult religious education which are important for the cultural context.

All cultures and spiritualities are both challenge and gift to the churches. The challenge to the churches and adult religious education is to critique the normative ways of Christian education, worship, justice, and spiritual leadership. The gift is that those churches which are open can be enriched in turn by another people's culture and spirituality.

Cultural factors are first supported when churches and religious educators respect the invitation to become part of a cultural community. The first step is to walk with the people, to work at genuinely understanding and appreciating who they are. Our North American tendency is to emphasize the individual. We must come to know the cultural community better. Each community has its own structure of relationships, its own dynamic of decision-making, and its own values and meaning-making rituals.

If our first step is the gentle walking with the people, then the people will see that our openness is honest and sincere. People will come to trust us and will be there. In one of our northern Native communities, the priest took years just walking wherever the people were, at their meetings or wherever, simply sharing their concerns, and their hopes. Today he is recognized as a spiritual person and they invite him to their traditional spiritual ceremonies. He does the same for the traditional spiritual leaders. Today he is being invited into gatherings that he would not even have known about if he had been naively overconfident about his role and place in the community. Another practical approach for the adult religious educator in the cultural context is to listen, and listen, and listen. One listens not only to the words being spoken, but also to the visions, the gestures, the rituals, and the symbols. It is very important to listen with more than the ears. I remember keenly wanting to be invited to one of the Native people's traditional ceremonies. I was getting frustrated with the fact that no one, even those I thought were receptive to outsiders and rather good friends, was inviting me. Then, one day, I recognized that the invitation had been there all along—it just was not spoken. Seemingly my initial desire was based on interest, not spiritual growth, and this blinded me from hearing (in the widest sense of that word) the spiritual invitation.

Another practical consideration in a cultural context is the need to discover and validate or to accept the unconventional methods of learning. There are alternative and effective ways of learning. Sometimes learners will say things like, "I don't have all the training you do," or "I don't know anything about that." In fact, they do know and they do learn, but in unconventional ways compared to the dominant society. Some people learn from dreams, intuition, and story-telling. I know some Native people who seriously discuss their dreams.

Native people are reclaiming their original spiritual vision from their elders and from their ancestors. Adult religious education must include the participation of the elders and provide open learning space (for example, silence, story-telling, or dreams) for the ancestors to speak. If rituals and stories have power to transform it is because the ancestors are present. However, today's approaches to adult education do not always respectfully include the wisdom of our elders or the presence of our ancestors. Adult religious education must include the elderly and those who have died before us—our ancestors.

The case study presented here focused on the Native peoples, specifically the Ojibway and Cree peoples. The practice of adult religious education happens in a cultural context. There is certainly a North American culture, but increasingly there is a growing awareness of the spiritual power and richness of all ethnic or cultural groups. The planning, practice, and evaluation of adult religious education must include cultural considerations. Some cultural considerations may be very evident. Most are not unless one is truly included in the community and is listening in the widest sense of the word. I was reminded recently how even the simple greeting of another person can communicate so much. A Ukrainian friend of mine said that someone in the Ukrainian community questioned why she simply said, "hello." If she had used the usual Ukrainian greeting, which varies according to the liturgical season, then the person would have been able to reply appropriately, and they both would have been living more spiritually. An outsider to this culture, by simply saying "hello," communicates to the Ukrainian person how he or she perceives spiritual or religious living—as being apart from daily circumstances, whereas those in the Ukrainian community view the everyday and the spiritual as being very closely linked. This simple greeting is culturally laden and needs to be understood by those working in this context.

Adult religious education, and the churches, can be very supportive as Native peoples, Afro-American/ Canadian, Hispanics, Vietnamese, Koreans, Ukrainians, and so forth, reclaim their original spiritual vision. As we live on mother earth and listen on a different path, we must be open to other spiritual traditions "so that our peoples may be blessed and God's creation healed." [29]

DISCUSSION QUESTIONS

1. What lessons can be learned from this case study? How can these lessons be applied to the cultural group that you work with?

2. Construct or relate your own case study based on the cultural group with which you work. How are the lessons from your study similar to the ones discussed in this chapter?

3. Many cultural groups are reclaiming their culture and spirituality. They are exercising self-government in many aspects of community life. How can adult religious education promote cultural groups' self-government over their own spiritual growth?

4. Community learning methods are important for spiritual learning. Identify the current methods you use for adult religious education. How much do they really reflect methods which promote community learning?

NOTES

1. Harold Cardinal, "Embarking upon a Sensitive, Painful and Troubling Task," *Home Mission* 10 (June, 1991), p. 11.

2. Douglas Crosby, O.M.I., "An Apology to the First Nations of Canada," *Kerygma* 25 (1991), p. 130.

3. These and subsequent figures are from Statistics Canada as reported by A. C. Hamilton and C. M. Sinclair (Eds). *The Justice System and Aboriginal People* (Winnipeg, Man.: The Queen's Printer, 1991), pp. 92-94.

4. Canadian Conference of Catholic Bishops, "Widespread Unemployment: A Call to Mobilize the Social Forces of Our Nation" (Ottawa, Ont.: CCCB Publications, 1992), p. 9.

5. See A. C. Hamilton and C. M. Sinclair, *The Justice System*, p. 68.

6. See George E. Tinker, *Missionary Conquest: The Gospel and Native American Cultural Genocide* (Minneapolis, Minn.: Fortress Press, 1993), p. 7.

7. Douglas Crosby, O.M.I., "An Apology," p. 130.

8. Robert F. Smith, from *The Apology* as found in the pamphlet entitled *In the Public Arena: Social Policy Positions of the United Church of Canada* (available from The United Church Bookstore, 120 Maryland, Winnipeg, Man.).

9. David Boud (Ed.), *Problem-Based Learning in Education for the Professions* (Sydney, Australia: Herdsa, 1985), p. 13.

10. Peter Hart, "The Future of the Church Among the Dene: Reflecting on Leadership Development," *Insight* 3 (1990), p. 24.

11. Arthur Solomon, in Michael Posluns' (Ed.), *Songs for the People* (Toronto, Ont.: New Canada Publications, 1991), p. 80.

12. The Dr. Jessie Saulteaux Resource Centre is in Beausejour, Manitoba, Canada, R0E 0C0.

13. The All Native Circle Conference is located at 18-399 Berry Street, Winnipeg, Manitoba, R3J 1N6.

14. For readings on inculturation see Archiel Peelman, *L'inculturation: L'église et les cultures* (Ottawa, Ont.: Novalis, University of St. Paul, 1988) and Vincent Donovan, *Christianity Rediscovered* (Maryknoll, New York: Orbis Books, 1983).

15. George E. Tinker, *Missionary Conquest*, p. 39.

16. This was an experience of the author during a cultural ritual.

17. Basil Johnston, "Kitchi-Manitou Has Given Us A Different Voice," *Home Mission* 10 (December, 1991), p. 27.

18. Basil Johnston, *Ojibway Heritage*, (Toronto, Ont.: McClelland and Stewart, 1984), p. 13.

19. Basil Johnston, p. 27.

20. This was taken from a story the author had heard in the Native community.

21. For more on the sacred circle see Kateri Mitchell, "Questions of Faith and Culture: Native Catechesis," *Caravan* 4 (Winter, 1991).

22. Basil Johnston, *Ojibway Heritage*, p. 61.

23. The term "ethic of non-interference" is taken from "Native Ethics and Rules of Behaviour" by Clare Brant, *Canadian Journal of Psychiatry* 35 (1990), p. 535.

24. See Individual Learning Covenants in R. E. Y. Wickett, *Models of Adult Religious Education Practice* (Birmingham, Ala.: Religious Education Press, 1991), pp. 128-151.

25. Ibid., pp. 100-110.

26. See Frank Adams with Myles Harton, *Unearthing Seeds of Fire: Highlander* (Winston-Salem, N.C.: John F. Blair, Publisher, 1975).

27. As reported by Dorothy Lachance in "Native Community Uses Holistic Model of Healing," *Prairie Messenger* 71 (September 6, 1993), p. 3.

28. For more information on the Community Holistic Circle of Healing either write CHCH Project, c/o Hollow Water, Manitoba, R0E 2E0, or read Catherine Mitchell, "Healing the Soul," *The Winnipeg Free Press* (April 8, 1991), p. 3.

29. Robert F. Smith, "The Apology," 1986.

ABOUT THE AUTHOR

J. Gregory Dunwoody is a layperson engaged in adult religious education, ministry training, and community development. He works primarily with the Saulteaux and Cree peoples in Manitoba. He also facilitates regional and national training sessions in adult religious education. Greg is a member of the Order of Mary Immaculate (O.M.I.) Resource Team, Winnipeg, Manitoba.

4. PASTORAL COUNSELING IN THE COMMUNITY

Ruth L. Wright

This chapter presents a view of pastoral counseling as part of the healing ministry of the church. This counseling must be shared among clerics and laity, both because there is theological grounding for the sharing and because of growing demands for pastoral energies. In the chapter an overview of the church's role in healing is presented. This role is a unique means of outreach as well as a unifying force within the community. The need for adequate levels of spiritual development, skill development, experience, and supervision are addressed.

If the ministry of the church is to expand to include the laity in more active roles, there is need for a serious effort to educate those persons who will be involved. The model of education which seems most appropriate, both in terms of the laity to be involved and the methodology which is affordable in a time of severe financial crisis, can be described best as adult religious education. This approach utilizes the facilities and the human resources available in an efficient and effective manner.

Through an understanding of the theoretical approach to pastoral counseling, one can understand better the practical demands for adult religious education in efforts to increase the role of the laity in the process. This chapter comprises three major sections. The first distinguishes between pastoral counseling and pastoral care in an effort to identify the realm of appropriate activities. Terms are defined, and a theological perspective is delineated which describes appropriate involvement of the laity in the counseling role of the church. This section also describes the parochial context. The second major section describes the development of community programs from a practical perspective. It includes practical aspects of training, skill development, and supervision. The third section reaffirms the role of pastoral counseling within adult religious education.

PASTORAL COUNSELING AS DISTINCT FROM PASTORAL CARING

The idea that Christianity is more a way of life than it is a matter of any particular creed or dogma is becoming more generally acknowledged by parishioners of most denominations in the 1990s. With that belief has come a partial renaissance in the manner in which churches and parishes are functioning. The predominating concern for the welfare of the individual is being replaced gradually by a more systemic view which purports that if any member suffers, the whole community suffers.

Accompanying this change of perspective is a questioning of the traditional differentiation between the role of the clergy and the role of the laity in worship, in ministering to one another, and in representing the will of God in the greater community. In some sense this trend can be seen in terms of the rediscovery of the Jewish roots of the Christian faith and the emerging recognition of God's care, not just for individuals but for the community as a whole and for all creation. As the laity become more involved with the worship activities of the church, they are becoming increasingly responsive to the need for representing their Christian principles in the community as a whole. The prophet's charge (in Micah 6:8) that we love mercy, do justice, and walk humbly with God has become the action mandate for many in the Christian church. This is expressed in many ways, such as Liberation Theology, Ecological Theology, and Feminist Theology. It has also been expressed by a growing sense of the need for more parishioners to become more actively involved in what has been deemed the domain of the clergy—pastoral counseling and pastoral care.

Definition

There have been many discussions of what makes pastoral counseling and pastoral care "pastoral."[1] Perhaps the most essential component for any definition of the term pastoral is that it incorporates and uses as a starting point a belief in Christ and an expectation that the Spirit of God is somehow involved in the interactions taking place. Pastoral work involves the acknowledgment of the grace of God as foundational to what happens in interactions among persons.

There is considerable controversy about the need to distinguish pastoral care from pastoral counseling. Richard Underwood, for example, maintains that pastoral care is "work of the representative ministry as it brings Christ to persons and celebrates the presence of Christ among people in interpersonal gatherings," whereas pastoral counseling is confined to "personal consultation with individuals or small groups, in which persons represent Christ and the ministry of the church and who serve in the context of a Christian congregation seek to help those whose celebration and conduct of life can in principle be engaged in dialogue with the Christian gospel."[2] What may be more important than the distinction for pastors and laity in small parishes is that some pastoral care is ongoing and well within the realm of the abilities of the persons involved, whereas much that is deemed counseling requires the skill of a trained psychologist or psychiatrist. All care and counseling that is pastoral is supported by and integrated in the recognition of God's grace, and is grounded in genuine caring authenticity.

The whole matter of authenticity is intertwined with issues of ethics. This issue is dealt with by Don Smith in his chapter in this book. Here, the fact that the essential component in a Christian understanding of God, that God is a God of grace, emerges. To be pastoral, counseling and care involves ethical confrontation and it is didactic. For the cleric a particularly thorny ethical issue emerges from the recognition that the "privilege of initiative"[3] is theirs, which allows them to enter the homes of parishioners and raise issues unbidden in a manner not normally available to non-clerics. On the other hand, this allows matters to be addressed which otherwise might not be confronted. The right of the individual to privacy may be violated, however, and the need for readiness for counseling may be ignored. Another important consideration is that the role of cleric generates a stereotypical view in some, which evokes the feeling of the need to appear to be pious, which may get in the way of counseling efforts.

Healing—A Scriptural Perspective

Pastoral care and pastoral counseling are both concerned with healing in the broadest sense of the word. The anticipated outcome of the counseling act is emotional, psychological, and spiritual healing. Throughout the biblical tradition, healing has been perceived to be the work of Yahweh and of the agents of Yahweh.[4] While the idea of healing as the work of Yahweh is generally a shared perspective, the source of illness is variously attributed to Yahweh, to the suffering person's own folly, to the evil of the ancestors of the ill person, or to other forces. How healing is accomplished, according to biblical writers, appears to have as much to do with the cultural setting in which they wrote as with any other factor.

All three sections of the Hebrew scriptures present an image of Yahweh as healer. The healing is present as a central aspect of God's covenant with the chosen people. The healing of Abilelech's wife and slaves from the infertility to which they were subjected as a result of being unfaithful to God is one example of sin-invoked illness. The Exodus (15:26) statement, "I am Yahweh your healer," exemplifies God's claim to the activity. Deuteronomy (32:31) states, "There is no other God beside me, I kill and I make alive; I wound and I heal." Healing is associated with forgiveness and with renewal of human spirits in many psalms.[5] The prophet Isaiah (6:10; 19:22) appealed to the

Israelites to turn back to God to be healed. (6:10; 19:22; 30:26) and Jeremiah (3:22) echoed the appeal to the people to return to God to receive healing. Ezekiel (34:4) rebuked Israel for its failure to care for the sick and the crippled, which he viewed as Yahweh's working through the people. God is viewed in these references as punishing with illness. Prophets, including Elijah (1 Kings 17:8-23) and Elisha (2 Kings 5:1-14) were described as agents of Yahweh in the healing act.

The Hebrew scriptures also depict cures for illness emerging from atoning sacrifices. The book of Leviticus (13, 14) directs the Israelites to be pure because there is a direct link between sickness and ritual impurity which only an atoning sacrifice can overcome. The role of physicians (and by extension, the role of psychiatrists and psychologists) was praised in some scripture (2 Chronicles 16:12) and described as useless in other scripture (Job 13:4).

Josephus credits some human illness to the work of demons, a theme adopted in the book of Tobit, which depicts the role of an angel named Raphael with the task of transmitting information to make possible cures and exorcisms. Josephus described part of Solomon's wisdom as including knowledge of the natural world and of the things which would safeguard humans from demons. The Dead Sea Scrolls also attribute human illness to demons. Greek culture obviously influenced these positions.

There was a more positive attitude toward physicians in the time of Jesus[6] but the adequacy of their methods was challenged. Some increased credence given to physicians by the New Testament writers is probably due, at least in part, to the fact that Luke, a chosen disciple, was a physician.

Large portions of the New Testament writings are devoted to descriptions of healing, particularly of the healing works of Jesus and their aftermath. Three verbs were used to describe the healings performed by Jesus: *hiaomai*—which means to cure or deliver from illness;

therapeuo—which means to wait upon, care for, or heal; and *sothesomai*—which means to restore and make whole.[7] In all of the healings Jesus performed, faith seems to have been an issue, either the faith of the person who was ill, or the faith of someone requesting healing. Much of Jesus' healing activity seems to have been an effort to demonstrate the priority of human health over the Jewish law. Jesus identified the source of his healing power as God, (Luke 5:17); others who used the name of Jesus also were able to heal.

Jesus frequently used the rites from the Jewish tradition in healing. Those who followed him used both anointing with oil and the laying on of hands in combination with rituals of prayer. Like Josephus, who described Old Testament healing as generating opportunities for worship, the disciples and New Testament Christians saw a vital link between healing and proclamation. Paul depicted the power to heal as one of the gifts of the Spirit and linked the healing of the sick with the proclamation of God's power (1 Corinthians 12:9-10; 29-30).

The anointing of the sick was a tradition that continued among Christians. Hippolytus reported the use of oil for application to the body and for drinking as early as A.D. 215. The tradition of the early Christians and of the early Roman Catholic Church, in particular, saw the ritual of anointing carried out in the family context with oil that had been blessed by a bishop. It was not until the Carolingian period, about A.D. 800, that there was a shift of emphasis toward presbyterial anointing, and even then, the clergy involvement was largely in regard to deathbed reconciliation. By the scholastic period, the anointing ritual was utilized almost exclusively at death. The anointing of the sick became viewed as the anointing for eternal life. The sacrament was considered to be related only to supernatural grace and not to bodily healing.[8]

The Council of Trent did not completely endorse the

spiritual reality of anointing. It was not until the Second Vatican Council that the sacrament of anointing was restored to express the power of Christ for all who were sick. Even in the post-Vatican II period, healing as a living ritual has been associated with particular sites for particular types of healing. Anointing as a part of worship has become more common in Protestant churches. There is a return, also, to laity involvement in the anointing process.

The New Testament church came to recognize the atoning role of Jesus and the liberating role of Christ. No longer was God considered to be completely outside the individual, but those who acknowledge the restoration of communion with God through the Christ were deemed to be indwelt with God's Spirit. Christians seek "the reign of God"—wholeness through Christ, or "the final realization of our ever incipient human wholeness—personal, social, cosmic—the communion of all human beings with each other and with God in Jesus Christ."[9] This means that as a church, our healing ministry, (our counseling ministry), must be comprehensive and must have at least three component parts: societal, medical, and pastoral.

The model for health in human persons is Christ whose "lordship" provides the paradigm for the fully human life. God is perceived as continually acting in a healing and restorative way and, as God's partners, humans apply reason and compassion toward healing, changing and sustaining the world as God's intention becomes clear.

The relationship between the Christian church and physicians also has changed over time. Where once physicians were looked on with skepticism, medical services to the community historically became associated with the church. Many communities continue to be served by church-sponsored hospitals and hospices. It was the work of medical missionaries in many communities that fostered the development of society as we know it. But in recent years, there has been a sharp schism between many in the medical community and many in the religious community, that has pitted one against the other. This is particularly true in highly technological societies.

The Parochial Context

Within a parish, parishioners hold the full spectrum of beliefs exhibited in the references made to the Hebrew scripture passages, to New Testament passages, to the early church, and to the incarnate view of God professed today. People who are in need of counseling are frequently described or describe themselves as deserving their illness, as causing their illness, as being "possessed," and/or as deserving to die. These feelings frequently result in fear, guilt, isolation and failure to seek the help and the support available through the Christian community. In a similar manner, some people perceive their own illnesses as "testing" and "strengthening" and take comfort in demonstrating their ability to be tested.

There is an increasing recognition in the church that any type of emotional, psychological, or spiritual need in one person has a profound affect on the church community, not just on the individual identified as in need. J. Glen notes that, "The work of healing, in the comprehensive Christian sense, falls not only to professional medical, social, and pastoral personnel but to all of us who are neighbour to the sick and their co-suffering families and friends."[10]

Counseling, from this perspective, is far more than a cure, it is the reconciliation of all the relationships disrupted by the need; it consists ultimately of the offer and acceptance of an "eschatological perspective as the ground upon which present relationships can be reconstructed toward a wholeness at every level in the trust and hope that they are the radical presence of the future coming into being in our midst."[11] It does not necessarily involve full recovery.

Rites are symbolic ways in which the church can

reclaim the reign of God. They are corporate symbolic actions that help give understanding to chaotic experiences. They help the community own the present and perceive it as bearable, but they also help the community claim the future hope that makes it possible and desirable. "Christian ritual in time of suffering is the Church's symbolic proclamation of the Christian eschatological vision offered for the Church's appropriation."[12] As such, rituals must articulate the tension that exists between hope and suffering, for, as Van der Poel suggests, "Suffering is not something to strive for, nor is it something to flee from.... Suffering is unavoidably human and needs to be healed, but healing itself is a process that leads to wholeness, to a wholeness found in God."[13]

Not all illness can be cured, not all pain can be healed, and not all counseling maintains life in our preferred form. The knowledge that death is near, for example, generates a significantly different set of reactions in people that are only beginning to be understood. The reactions of persons in need of emotional and spiritual healing are less well understood. Nevertheless, there are some practical approaches toward developing community programs.

DEVELOPING COMMUNITY PROGRAMS

In developing community programs, three factors are important to consider: parish size, methodology of training and skill development, and supervision of the program.

Practical Considerations of Parish Size

It would be overly simplistic to suggest only that pastoral counseling should and could be a shared ministry among the clerics and laity. Careful planning and education are required to develop a program which might be of help in a parish. Not everyone should or could be formally involved in such a scheme and it might do more harm than good to the church's outreach for some parishioners to become part of such a formal program.

There is, however, a growing need for pastoral counseling resulting from changing societal conditions which the church can not afford to ignore. Increasing unemployment, mushrooming numbers of family breakdowns, the demise of the middle class, and the burgeoning numbers of poor in every community demand a response from the Christian community which speaks of the power of the Christ it proclaims. A Christian response demands involvement; that is, a significant radical involvement of the Christian community.

In small rural parishes which characterize so much of North America, the pastor has limited resources available to assist in the training of persons for an appropriate level of involvement in the counseling process. It is also almost impossible to have parishioners travel to other centers or to import persons for the training that is necessary for anything other than supportive care and counseling.[14] Yet, having a cadre of persons with even this skill level as part of the church's ministry has a profound impact on the ministry of the parish.

> If the aim of pastoral counseling, and indeed churches in general, is the formation of communities of people willing to love and care for their world, and to challenge those who would exploit rather than care, then a force for social change is implicitly grounded in pastoral counseling itself.[15]

It may be that the pastor has to assume responsibility for the basic instruction in the skills, or that the pastor in association with other professionals from the area may be jointly responsible for planning the training sessions.

Training and Skill Development

Three major areas of skill development should be addressed in any counseling program: attending, responding, and assessing.[16] These are basic communication skills. They involve learning to listen in a manner which pays attention not only to what is being said, but how it is said, so as to elicit further information, and in learning to identify the cues which signal the need for further action. Training in these skills involves modelling, role playing, and practice. Specifically, attending involves skills in positioning, observing, and listening. Responding includes skills of paraphrasing, identifying feelings, and probing for additional relevant information. Assessing incorporates skills in summarizing what has been said, or left unsaid, identifying hunches, eliciting feelings, and demonstrating a caring presence. Each of these skills can be learned in many contexts with minimal feedback. Practice in the skills and ongoing feedback in their development is critical to their effective use, but the feedback can be from other learners as well as from the pastor responsible for training. Learning and using these skills will help almost anybody to be able to give effective supportive counsel.

Having skills is only part of the counseling process. Knowing when one is capable of giving appropriate counsel becomes something less able to be taught directly than other skills. Issues of consultation, collaboration, and referral need to be paramount considerations in efforts to educate pastoral counselors in the community. M. M. Cunningham, B. B. Rader, and M. F. Hughes-McIntyre each describe issues of ethics, personal identity, sensitivity to self and to others, personal experience and growth, reporting, psychological theories and under-standing; and of power which must be addressed by individuals during training,[17] and also during their subsequent practice of their counseling skills as members of a parish team. Training activities in these areas can include group discussions of issues, direct instruction, reading assignments, self-scored tests, films and videos, and any number of combinations of these. It is important, however, that the pastor meet regularly with those persons formally involved in the process, in order to assess their competence in these areas.

All the practical matters mentioned are relevant to any type of community-based counseling program designed to develop persons with abilities to provide supportive counsel. The pastoral element of such a program has not been considered, and although it might include some of the learnings which are denominational-specific, it needs to be particularly concerned with the level of spiritual development of the counselor and the person or persons to be counseled.

There are many descriptions of stages of faith development; all have their strengths and limitations. One of the most popular, and consequently most criticized, is proposed by James Fowler.[18] Four assumptions underlie his theory. The first is that human beings are potentiated for partnership with God. The second is that humans are created with the genetic potential for relationships with God and with one another. The third is that our culture and shared social meaning determines, in large part, who we are and who we become. The fourth assumption is that we learn to reflect and to be aware of ourselves gradually through a sequence of developmental constructs.

Although the stages of faith development are not limited to age categories, they do seem to develop in a consistent sequence. The first stage, intuitive-projective faith, is typical of young children. It is characterized by the ability to form strong images presented in stories but to understand the images mostly in terms of taboos and doctrinal expectations. The second stage, mythical-literal faith, is characterized by individuals appropriating beliefs, stories, and observations that symbolize belonging to community. This includes the understanding of reciprocal relationships within the community of faith. The third stage, synthetic-conventional faith, is characterized by the person structuring the environment in interpersonal terms, and this typically leads to conformist behavior because the test of reality is in terms of the reaction of others. The fourth stage is individuate-reflective faith. In this stage the myths of faith become personally meaningful and a personal theology develops through critical reflection, rather than primarily from the reactions of others. The fifth stage is called conjunctive faith. In this stage a person is able to reassess the past and make sense of it at a deeper level. It results in a deeper understanding of identity and can result in a much stronger social conscience, often through dialectical processes. The sixth stage, universal faith, is still viewed as hypothetical. It is a stage in which questions of faith are approached from a universal rather than a particular perspective.[19]

Having a sense of the level of spiritual development as well as of the skill development of the counselor allows an appropriate pastoral match to be made. It is only when the counseling relationship leads to theological assessment, proclamation, and guidance that the counseling is pastoral.[20] This may be the area of most payoff for the parish, because as potential counselors become more aware of their level of spiritual development, they become more aware of their personal needs for spiritual development. The training and development of workers in this area is an ongoing process; it can be accomplished through group study sessions, through counseling of the counselors, and through encouraging self-development. Not everyone will achieve even stage four, but to know where a counselor is spiritually is to be able to know where they are likely to be effective as spiritual counselors (one can never discredit the possibilities of the Holy Spirit, however!). This is similar to knowing their level of skill development in other areas which suggests where they can be utilized most effectively.

Supervision of the Program

Although it is helpful to have assistance in pastoral counseling in a parish, there is an obligation to supervise the pastoral counseling that is occurring. In a small parish that duty is part of the pastor's task; it is integral to the effective ministry of the church. Supervision has long been associated with negative feelings—those being supervised often feel they are being spied upon, or not trusted. But supervision goes beyond administrative management in a program of pastoral counseling to include a therapeutic dimension. It then focuses on the personal growth of the counselor, and a dimension of a working alliance which is part of the building of the community of the church.[21] In pastoral counseling the supervisory practice is a more important activity than in many other areas of ministry, because there is so much at stake—people's lives, the faith, the church community.

It is the supervisory practice which insures that inappropriate persons are not involved in the formal pastoral counseling process of the church. It is the supervisory process that helps the pastor identify with the counselor the areas in which further developments are needed. It is the supervisory process that allows opportunities for the identification of alternative delivery systems both for training and for counseling. It is the supervisory system that allows a program to survive when a pastor moves to another parish. Every program forms part of a larger picture.

PASTORAL COUNSELING AS ADULT RELIGIOUS EDUCATION

It has been argued that there is a type of counseling that is truly "pastoral" and that this counseling is and should be a role both of clergy and laity in a Christian community. Pastoral counseling is a form of ministry which incorporates rites and rituals of the faith and which reflects the theology of both the Hebrew scriptures and New Testament tradition. It has also been acknowledged that the current level of understanding of what is effective pastoral counseling is rudimentary, but that such a healing ministry is a shared ministry which must be attentive to not only spiritual dimensions of people's needs, but to physical and interactional dimensions.

Pastoral counseling is an integral part of the church's ministry, particularly in times of societal crises, such as our own. It is a time-intensive part of ministry and demands far more than the normal capabilities of most pastors in most parishes. Christian theology acknowledges the role of all Christians in caring for its members; that care can extend to supportive counseling.

There are particular skills which are critical to good counseling of any type. These skills can be learned to some level by most people and, when utilized properly, they can be integral to the formal counseling program of the parish. There is, however, a distinguishing characteristic of pastoral counseling—it is theologically based. This characteristic makes it particularly important to the church's mission. The level of spiritual development of counselors is a determining factor in their ability to provide counseling which is pastoral, and that should therefore be an integral consideration in their assignment to counseling tasks.

Pastoral counseling is one part of the ministry of the church and as such should be administered in a manner consistent with the other areas of ministry in the community. The type of integration which allows a pastoral counseling program requires careful supervision to be effective.

The development of a cadre of pastoral counselors in a parish is an educational task, and a task to be taken seriously. It requires careful attention to skill identification, skill development, practice, feedback, and ongoing education in knowledge areas. The knowledge and utilization of effective adult learning principles in the development of skilled pastoral counselors is critical to the task.

DISCUSSION QUESTIONS

1. Think about your own parish. How much need is there for pastoral counseling which is not being met by the pastor? How critical do you view this need? Why?

2. What factors in the community are creating the need for pastoral care? How many of those factors could be influenced by the church community?

3. As you think of your parish, identify the people you know who might make good contributions to the pastoral counseling program of your church. What do you think they might need to help them feel confident in being part of a pastoral counseling team?

4. How do you view pastoral counseling as different from other types of counseling? What faith issues would you want addressed if you were to become part of such a team?

5. What resources (people and material) are available in your parish which might be helpful in developing a community pastoral counseling team?

NOTES

1. The works of H. J. Clinebell and G. E. Whitlock are classics in this area. Most textbooks concerned with pastoral counseling or pastoral care present some operational definition of "pastoral."

2. R. L. Underwood, "Pastoral Counseling in the Parish Setting," in *Clinical Handbook of Pastoral Counseling*, ed. R. J. Wicks, R. D. Parsons, and D. Capps (New York: Paulist Press, 1985), pp. 333-334.

3. W. B. Oglesby, *Biblical Themes for Pastoral Care*. (Nashville, Tenn.: Abingdon, 1980); see especially, pp. 45-77.

4. H. Kee, "Medicine and Healing," in *The Anchor Bible Dictionary*, Volume 4, ed. D. Freedman (New York: Doubleday), pp. 659-664.

5. See particularly Psalms 41:4; 30:2; 103:3; 107:19-20.

6. See, for example, Matthew 9:12; Mark 2:17; Luke 5:31.

7. H. Kee, p. 660.

8. W. Cuenin, "History of Anointing and Healing in the

Church," *Alternative Futures for Worship*, volume 7, pp. 65-81.

9. J. Glen, "Rite of Healing: A Reflection in Pastoral Theology," *Alternative Futures for Worship*, 7, p. 45

10. Ibid., p. 47.

11. Ibid., p. 47.

12. Ibid., p. 50.

13. C. Van der Poel, "Suffering and Healing: The Process of Growth," in *The Ministry of Healing: Readings in the Catholic Health Care Ministry* (St. Louis, Mo: Catholic Health Association of the United States, 1981), pp. 43-54.

14. H. J. Clinebell, *Basic Types of Pastoral Care and Counseling* (Burlington, Ont.: Welsh Publishing, 1989).

15. C. J. Steckel, "Directions in Pastoral Counseling," in *Clinical Handbook of Pastoral Counseling*, ed. Wicks, Parsons and Capps, pp. 26-36.

16. C. W. Taylor, *The Skilled Pastor: Counseling as the Practice of Theology* (Minneapolis: Fortress Press, 1991).

17. M. M. Cunningham, "Consultation, Collaboration and Referral," in *Clinical Handbook of Pastoral Counseling*, ed. Wicks, Parsons, and Capps, pp. 162-170; B. B. Rader, "Supervision of Pastoral Psychotherapy," in *The Organization and Administration of Pastoral Counseling Centers*, eds. J. C. Carr, J. E. Hinckle and D. M. Moss (Nashville, Tenn., Abingdon, 1981), pp. 78-89; and M. F. Hughes-MacIntyre, "Theory of Supervision of Pastoral Counseling," *Journal of Supervision and Training in Ministry*, 4, pp. 63-74.

18. J. Fowler has written several books related to this topic. *Faith Development and Pastoral Care* (Philadelphia: Fortress Press, 1987) is probably the most relevant for this discussion.

19. J. Fowler, *Stages of Faith: The Psychology of Human Development and the Quest for Meaning* (San Francisco: Harper & Row, 1981).

20. C. W. Taylor, pp. 61-135.

21. D. A. Steere, *The Supervision of Pastoral Care* (Louisville, John Knox, 1989).

ABOUT THE AUTHOR

Ruth L. Wright is Associate Professor of Educational Administration at the University of Ottawa, in Ottawa, Ontario. She holds a masters degree in Curriculum Theory and a doctorate in Educational Administration. She has been a consultant to several school boards, and on national and international curriculum projects. Currently pastor of Zion United Church in Apple Hill, Ontario, she is a candidate for ordained ministry in The United Church of Canada.

PART III

IMPROVING PRACTICE IN ADULT RELIGIOUS EDUCATION

As the pace of change quickens in all disciplines, adult religious educators are challenged even more to engage constantly in the task of improving practice. Since practice is often bettered through theory and research, this section attempts to look at four areas of interest that are very important to the future development of adult religious education. Each topic provides specific suggestions on how to improve local community practice by examining the impact of the current literature and research. As church agencies and institutions continue to develop programs, it is important to emphasize that helping people discover the journey of faith development is as natural as life itself, and that this discovery is at the heart of improving the field of practice.

One of the key ingredients of a training program is a sound philosophical foundation. Marge Denis and Brenda Peddigrew tell us that preparing to be an adult religious educator involves both a short-term and long-term dedication to a way of life rather than to a job or role. In a condensed manner they offer a training program for someone who wishes to become an adult religious educator. At the heart of the program is "The Person of the Adult Religious Educator" with "Interactive Techniques" making a bridge to "The Person of the Adult Learner" and finally the linking to "Content."

In the second chapter, R. Wickett and M. Freitag suggest that a faith journey is sustained by many things including the process of learning. Faith development, therefore, involves a journey that requires learning and relevant resources to sustain it. Their chapter is concerned with the widest possible range of resources for many purposes involving learning. Both human and material resources are included. Human resources discussed include peers, educators and community members while material resources focus in on electronic, textual and distance education.

As program delivery expands in the field of adult religious education, the notion of self-directed learning is gaining momentum. In his chapter René Bédard explains how self-directed learning has the potential to improve practice in adult religious education. He traces the development of this phenomenon through different educational fields and illustrates how such an approach can provide opportunities to promote both religious and spiritual experiences. He also suggests that this process of learning has great potential for adults who are interested in continued growth.

As issues in this new field continue to surface, authenticity and ethics in adult religious education are receiving more and more attention. Don Smith explains throughout his chapter that authenticity and ethics means adult educators participate in the development of the knowledge, skills and attitudes of adult learners in order to perceive the world through their eyes. He argues that authenticity and ethics can be viewed as principles for learning and that stewardship or service leadership is the new approach to adult education. The chapter is forthright and contains current thinking from the field of organizational learning.

Threaded throughout this section, the theme of linking research with practice has emerged. Common to all chapters is the fact that knowledge about the adult learner and the principles of the learning process is crucial for improving practice in adult religious education. Programs and activities that recognize the wholeness of learners and respect their educational backgrounds and personal experiences enable participants to become actively involved in their journey of faith development.

1. PREPARING TO FACILITATE ADULT RELIGIOUS EDUCATION

Marge Denis and Brenda Peddigrew

The nature of adult religious education highlights the most basic truths affecting human existence. Given this understanding, the adult religious educator is a person who lives from and dialogues with these basic truths every day, and who searches for ways to facilitate how others engage in the same dialogue. Preparing to be an adult religious educator, then, involves both short-term and long-term dedication to a way of life rather than to a job or a role.

The person of the adult religious educator is the heart and center of this chapter, for although we recognize many available sources on the "what" and the "how" of adult religious education, we notice very little being spoken about the "who." Our chapter offers a condensed training program for someone who wishes to become an adult religious educator. Lastly, the content involved in a training program forms the outer circle farthest from the center. We place less emphasis on this element in educator preparation because it is the most easily acquired and it is the element most subject to change. Our purpose in this chapter is to be as practical as possible; the theory we present is thus operational, and is not offered for its own sake. In proceeding with this work, we wish to clarify several assumptions that form the basis for our convictions in this area.

SOME WORKING ASSUMPTIONS

First, we assume adult religious education to be a personal interaction between the adult religious educator and the adult learner in a given context. The imparting of information is not primary in this exchange, though it might be a part of it. Rather, the heart of this personal interaction flows from the heart of Christianity—the great commandment to "love your neighbor as yourself." All else in adult religious education—skills, content, planning—must be grounded in this kind of personal interaction.

Our second assumption involves the nature of learning. Learning is change. Learning is living. Acquiring facts or information is important but it is not at the core of adult religious education. Such acquisition can be accomplished without any change of heart. The gospel call is to "fullness of life" (John 10) and this implies that the whole person—body, mind, spirit/soul—is considered to be the focus of adult religious education.

The third underlying assumption of our approach to adult religious education is the belief that it is important to avoid jargon relating to school, which has very specific and limited connotations for adults. *Learning* is not a "school" word; we refer to *adult learners* rather than *adult students*. We also strongly prefer the term *facilitator* rather than *teacher*, since it carries none of the weight of the hierarchical implications still defined by the word teacher.

Fourth, adult religious education is more than the education of adults, in the traditional academic understanding of that term. Adult religious education is a philosophy, an approach to learning, a way of being. Age boundaries are less important; children and the elderly would just as readily benefit from this approach to facilitating religious education, especially with its grounding in life issues and the understanding that to learn is to change.

Our fifth and final operational assumption relates to the context of our endeavor. Adult religious education is an invitation to grow and to change in the context of church and society. Community, prayer ritual, and a spiritual life are essential to the enterprise. No learner is an island.

THE PERSON OF THE ADULT RELIGIOUS EDUCATOR

The belief that adult religious education is more a way of life than a role to be played implies some recognizable characteristics of the person who chooses to live and work as an adult religious educator. The skills, the content, and the formal education in this field are important, but we believe that what is most important is to be grounded in oneself. This grounding has at least four dimensions that are meaningful here.

The first of these dimensions is *knowing one's assumptions*. When we began to write this chapter we realized, for example, that we were shaping our knowledge of adult religious education based on certain assumptions which we then made an effort to articulate at the beginning of this chapter. You might ask yourself, what are your own assumptions, as an adult religious educator, about, for example, the learners. Do you see them as ignorant? Smarter than you? Do you see yourself as knowing more than the learners? Are you assuming that learning will/will not take place? And what are your assumptions about church in this context? These questions are just the beginning of a list of assumptions that highly influence our work in adult religious education, and that influence it all the more when they are not named. Out of our assumptions, we act. If assumptions are hidden, especially from ourselves, they are dangerous. We recommend that you consider keeping an assumptions sheet, an ongoing log of noticing what you are assuming about people and situations that affect your life and work.

The second dimension of the person who is an adult religious educator relates to personal process. Process is the dynamic movement of growth and change characterizing all living organisms, including ideas and groups as well as individuals and created things. A competent facilitator has *the ability to recognize process in oneself*. This capacity for self-reflection is inherent in every human person, and can be developed using certain skills and techniques. Yielding to the ebb and flow of one's own developing life process enables the adult religious educator to acknowledge the same dynamic evolution not only in other persons but also in groups, in organizations, and in the whole of the created universe. Rooted in such an understanding, the adult religious educator designs very different approaches to her or his work than one who operates from a static and compartmentalized view of human-created and other-created reality. Recognizing process in oneself is fundamental, in our view, to preparing to be an adult religious educator.

The third dimension that is pertinent here is a natural outgrowth from the first two, namely, *claiming personal authority*. This dimension of living as an adult religious educator is sometimes frightening and very often risky for people who work in the context of churches with absolute teachings and beliefs; yet it is also necessary to maintain a creative tension between the individual and the organization if the teachings are to remain significant and helpful to the people who live by them. As a colleague of ours often says, "The church needs a loyal opposition." Failure on the part of adult religious educators to claim authority from within by respecting their own questions and concerns can contribute to a situation of absolute power that is dangerous in any organization. In churches, however, it is even more dangerous, because it is supported by spiritual teaching. The need for adult religious educators to claim personal authority is crucial to the important work of adult religious education.

The final dimension that we feel to be significant in the person of the adult religious educator addresses the fear to which we referred in the preceding paragraph, the fear of claiming personal authority. This dimension leads the person from the solid grounding in self, with which we began, to the necessary movement outward. We call this movement the *balancing of inner and outer processes*. Knowing one's assumptions, recognizing process in oneself, and claiming personal authority all form a habitat for dialogue, for creating a new reality by negotiating truths and mediating differences. Such an educator is empowered, and empowers others. The person of the adult religious educator is not complete without the presence of both knowing inner process and working with the outer processes of individuals, groups, and the churches who form her or his living environment.

THE PERSON OF THE LEARNER

A major consideration in preparing to facilitate adult religious education is our understanding of the person of the adult learner. What do we assume about adult learners? How do we view adult learning? How has our knowledge of learning changed over the years? How do we practice concretely what we understand learning and the learner to be? How aware are we of the cultural and social pressures existing for adult learners in particular situations? Social influences affect profoundly the quality of learning that takes place, and in our time the work of adult religious education seeks its way through realities such as unemployment, family violence, and the welfare cycle. Emotionally charged issues like homophobia and abortion make the path of adult religious education a treacherous one. Respecting the faiths of other people, with all their cultural implications, raises the fear of diminishing one's own faith through what has been called the watering-down process. And how does one deal with AIDS when it takes on the face of someone in an adult religious education learning group? This section responds to some of these questions arising from our experience in the field of adult religious education over many years. We outline six principles that have emerged for us as being fundamental to the practice of adult religious education, and after each one we name some of the conditions that foster this principle in more specific circumstances. We also include in this section ways in which we have come to recognize and respect how adults learn. We believe that the following principles are always present in good practice. We also include some concrete conditions that enhance the principles in their particular settings.

The Principles and Conditions of Adult Learning

1. *Learning is an interior process that is activated and controlled by the learner.* Education is primarily about learning, not teaching. This is a perspective that has often been lost, with undue emphasis being placed on methods of teaching rather than on the question, "what is going on inside these learners around me?" A humbling thought for a facilitator is this quote from an article by Pine and Horne,[1] "No one directly teaches anyone anything of significance." Every person has a unique learning style; the fallacy is that any learning can be imposed. We have only to recall our own experience of formal learning to recognize that, in most cases, we have forgotten the content of what had to be studied for examinations and we have retained only what had personal meaning for us. This realization alone invites us to name learning as a deeply spiritual activity that honors the uniqueness of every learner; the first concern about learners needs to be leaving people free to explore the ideas that are significant to them. A number of conditions foster this principle; two of these are:

• design learning experiences and activities that openly promote the freedom of the learner; and
• choose approaches that will deliberately respect the person of the learners in ways that enhance self-esteem and self-confidence.

2. *Learning is emotional and intuitive as well as intellectual and rational.* Congruent with one of our previously stated assumptions, that "learning is living; learning is change," we find that openly making a place for feelings in the learning process enhances the quality of learning and enables the learner to relate what is learned to her or his own life. Fear, for example, is a significant factor in

how or even whether people learn at all. Physical discomfort or limitations are others.

Consciously working with these and other feelings that affect the learner's ability to enter into the learning process clears the way for learning to take place. It also better ensures that the learning will be useful and lasting for the learners. A holistic understanding of the human person, respecting the equal value of the body, the mind, and the spirit and their interconnections, is an important consideration in the design of the learning experience. Two conditions fostering this principle are:

- giving time for the expression of feelings around an idea or task at hand; and
- encouraging people to be active, not passive, learners, taking responsibility for their learning, and to ask their own questions and form their own answers without your giving judgment or negative criticism.

3. *Learning (change) is a consequence of experience.* People need to experience what is being taught. Change does not come about simply by being told about something; rather, it occurs only when experience opens our hearts to the truth and, as a consequence, we can act differently. Doing affects being. In learning, then, we don't just tell, we don't just give information; more than that, we enable learners to engage with the teaching. For example, learning about prayer could include large bodies of information on the history of prayer, the forms of prayer, the prayer traditions of different religions, but it would not necessarily invite people to pray. Prayer is learned only by praying, just as theology does not necessarily invite an encounter with God, but is meant to be an intellectual study about God. Informational resources—for example, books, tapes and films—are important in any area of learning, but the richest resource for learning is the learner. What is essential is to encourage people to trust their own thought and their own experience. Conditions that foster this principle are:

• using problem-solving and discussion groups which create an environment that gives high value to an individual's discovery of the personal meaning of ideas; and

• enabling people to express their needs in the adult religious education setting, rather than telling them what their needs are.

4. *Learning is communal and social as well as individual and personal.* A climate of interdependence in which the learners recognize their need of one another is the style of facilitation we recommend here. Collaboration in the immediate learning task is consciously fostered; competition is given no place in this way of learning.

A further elaboration of this principle in the area of adult religious education is that it models the awareness that all of our learning affects the conditions of justice/injustice in our society and in our world. Learning in this way causes us to reflect and to act differently in our relationships with the systems that order all the aspects of our daily life. A condition that fosters this principle is:

• creating an ambiance in which learners become comfortable with feedback from one another as well as from the facilitator and in which each person accepts her or his place in a participative decision-making process.

5. *Learning is sometimes a painful process.* All that we have been naming in this section as basic to learning can be painful for people—for example, being open with others about our feelings and attitudes, taking risks in groups, confronting, being confronted, and changing our attitudes and our behaviors. In this principle of adult learning our experience teaches us that there is almost always resistance to growth and change and that the resistance also has meaning. Resistance often signals the last threshold before expansion into a new understanding, if we can stay with and move through the resistance. In Christian terms, we are speaking here of the

paschal mystery, that there is no resurrection (expansion into a new life, learning) without death (feeling the pain of our limited understanding). A caution regarding this principle that we feel necessary to name here is that a facilitator need not (indeed, must not) deliberately set out to create learning situations in which pain happens. This would be using a manipulative and destructive approach. The pain we are speaking about here is the natural pain endemic to the growth process, the pain that is common to all of us as human beings. We do wish to say, however, that it is crucial that the facilitator not shy away from the pain that is part of the learning process. A condition fostering this principle is:

• acknowledging the ambiguity of learning; when pain and discomfort are present in a group, it is more important to explore them rather than to ignore them or explain them too quickly.

Ways in Which Adults Learn

There have been various ways of looking at how people learn. We have found the work of David Kolb[2] to be the most useful. Kolb's research on how adults learn shows us that people prefer to learn in at least four different ways. These are:

1. By *concrete experience*. These people learn best by feeling and sensing what is new to them.
2. By *reflective observation*. These people learn best by watching and thinking about it.
3. By *abstract conceptualization*. These people learn best by naming and conceptualizing.
4. By *active experimentation*. These people learn best by doing, by trying things out. Some say that they don't know if they've learned something until they actually do it.

Abstract conceptualization is only one of four styles of learning, although it is the learning style with which we are most familiar. However, only a few people prefer to learn this way. Still, it is the way that has been valued primarily in our formal educational systems. Indeed, people who find it difficult to learn abstractly have often been made to feel inferior in our systems. Preferring a particular learning style doesn't mean that one is unable to learn in other ways, only that it is more difficult and takes more energy. Learning is a combination of all four learning styles, and it is important for adult religious educators to design learning experiences in which all four learning preferences are included.

If, as adult religious educators, we take account of all this knowledge about adult learners, how does it affect our approach? The next section of this chapter explicates the immediate preparations for facilitating adult religious education.

FACILITATING GROUP DEVELOPMENT

Several techniques interact with one another to form a tapestry of skills to be consciously learned as immediate preparation for facilitating adult religious education. We have grouped them under the following headings: facilitating, planning, establishing a learning climate, communicating well, and managing conflict.

At the beginning of working with any group, a facilitator is equally concerned with two types of issues: those of task and those of maintenance of relationships. *Task* issues focus on the reason that this group came together in the first place (its purpose) or the task that this group wishes to accomplish. The facilitator's initial concern around task involves designing the structures that will enable the group to be clear about roles, responsibilities and activities that enable the task to be accomplished. *Maintenance* issues focus on the relationships within the group; those between the facilitator and group members and those among members themselves. The facilitator finds ways to initiate and nurture open communication of feelings and reactions and to offer emotional support as group members begin to know one another. The facilitator notices tensions arising in the group and knows how to manage them effectively. Conflict is destructive to any group development, and therefore avoiding conflict is important.

The phrase *group maturity*, often found in the literature on group development, does not in any way refer to the maturity of individual group members, but only to how well this group is able to achieve the task for which it has been formed. Achieving the task effectively is influenced by these factors: ability to work together effectively; clarity about motivations and assumptions; the skill and the experience of group members as related to this specific task; and the degree of willingness among group members to take responsibility for achieving its purpose.

The maturing process of any group can usually be observed as progressing through four distinct phases. In each phase the facilitator's emphasis on task and/or relationship changes, with the degree of emphasis fluctuating according to the needs of the group in each phase.

Every group is initially immature in its beginning stage. This phase is characterized by the insecurity of group members as they get to know one another and begin to gauge for themselves how the task will be accomplished. The facilitator respects this time in the group's beginning by emphasizing task issues more than relationship issues; group members want to know clearly what the task is and how its achievement will come about. We call this first phase the "gimme" stage and the facilitator responds to the legitimate "gimme" needs of the group by providing input and clear structures for the way in which the group works together.

In the second phase of group development, members begin to actually work together and simultaneously encounter differences among themselves relating to the task at hand. These differences often amount to difficulties and even conflict in this early phase and they precipitate what we call the "gripe" stage. This period in the group's growth challenges the facilitator to attend equally to both task and relationship issues, and to give concentrated attention to both. The danger is that some groups become fixated in their griping and their purpose for being together can be lost.

When the group accepts responsibility for its task, and is working more effectively together, it has moved to what we call the "grope" stage of development. Members no longer need to be given great amounts of specific information or direction from the facilitator and their conflicts do not occupy center stage in the group's life. The facilitator needs to lessen her or his emphasis on task at this time, and to give it over to the group to the degree that they show willingness to take it. In this way, the facilitator empowers the group to own its task, and as a result can consider more attentively the dynamics of relationships within the group.

In the final phase of development, a group becomes mature—that is, its motivation is highly consistent; responsibility for the task and for maintaining relationships are almost entirely within the group; and members are clearly able to work together effectively and to deal with their own problems within the group. We call this stage the "grasp" phase, and it is rare indeed. The facilitator is only minimally needed here, if at all, and her/his challenge is to withdraw control at the appropriate moments, delegating both task and maintenance issues to the group itself.

"Gimme," "Gripe," "Grope," and "Grasp" express for us the cycle of group development that we have observed among all the groups with whom we have worked. It is helpful to practice identifying in which phase a group might be at a given time to glean direction for oneself as facilitator.

Facilitating Techniques

In the work of facilitation, questioning appropriately is a skill to be learned and an art to be developed with practice. Two points about questions are salient for a facilitator in any field: (a) the use of questioning requires advance planning; and (b) the knowledge of how to ask questions is essential.

Advance planning for questions necessitates clarity about the goals and objectives of the task at hand. Out of this clarity, questions can be prepared that relate directly to the goals and objectives, thereby furthering their achievement in a more focused way. Preparing questions carefully is also important because the nature and framing of questions affects the self-esteem of individuals in any situation. Advance planning does not mean that questions will be stilted or forced; it can be done so that the questions appear spontaneous, if they have been worded in accord with the heart of what is happening in a group and in accord with the level of challenge appropriate to this group.

One way to ascertain the stance of a group regarding a particular topic is to begin with a general question with many possible answers which, though not simplistic, challenges the learners and ensures initial success. Effective questions appear to be simple yet take a long time to formulate. A helpful practice for the facilitator is to test out questions on a colleague.

In *knowing how to ask questions,* we remind ourselves of some simple directions. For example, we need to speak clearly. We need to be brief, concise, to the point, honing our questions to sentences rather than paragraphs. A question requiring thought should be asked at least three times, paraphrasing each one differently so that feeling, thinking, and sensing perspectives are each respected. And we need to make sure that these are not three different questions!

Another important consideration is to work with the fear of silence, both within oneself and within the group.

Cultivating a respect for silence often allows for truer responses from the group, as we try together to become more comfortable with waiting for an answer. Then, when answers come, the facilitator needs to find a way to acknowledge each one positively. One simple way to practice this is to use *and* instead of *but* when responding to an answer that feels slightly off the mark or incomplete. For example, "Yes, I appreciate your answer, and..."

Finally, it is important to avoid *yes/no* questions. Their appropriate use is extremely limited, and in a group process setting yes/no questions ensure that the process itself will grind to an undesired halt.

Basic Learning Processes

Because learning takes place inside the learner, certain processes or dynamics are basic—that is, if these processes do not take place, learning does not happen. Professor Virginia Griffin[3] has researched and described these interior processes which we believe to be the core of facilitation. The A, B, Cs of these processes are:

A. Keeping centered and maintaining self-esteem;
B. Becoming responsible for increasing aspects of your own learning;
C. Discovering what you hope to learn (and realistically can learn) from participating in the course or event;
D. Getting involved, investing your energy, committing yourself;
E. Developing the most productive relations with others in the course;
F. Helping the group develop into an effective learning group;
G. Being open to new ideas, information, perspectives; giving up outdated perspectives and ideas;
H. Finding your meaning in the context and experiences; creating your own observations and generalizations;

I. Finding, understanding, testing your own ideas against the external information and ideas;

J. Naming, clarifying, consolidating, and synthesizing what you are learning;

K. Trying out new skills, behaviors, and ways of being;

L. Asking for and using others' feedback on your new (or old) skills, behaviors, and ways of being;

M. Anticipating use and using your new learning in other places;

N. Finding and accepting satisfaction, rewards, and results;

O. Identifying energy area for later learning; and

P. Clarifying, negotiating expectations, norms, and values.

If the facilitator consciously activates these processes in the learner around any given subject matter, learning will happen. These basic processes are both very profound and very simple.

Right Brain/Left Brain Activities

In the introduction to this chapter, we stated our belief that "learning is living" and "learning is change," and that our basic practice affirms a holistic approach to facilitating learning experiences. One way that we practice this belief is to consciously draw on the resources of what science has lately called the right brain to create a better climate for a whole-brain learning experience. Learning and education in the Western cultures has leaned heavily, often exclusively, on the gifts of the left brain, and we believe that this denial of right-brain functioning has contributed to the paralysis of change-ability when knowledge is before our very eyes. The special areas in which the right brain contributes to the whole picture are the following: seeing connections between things; synthesizing; recognizing likenesses between things; making metaphors; relating to things as they are in the present moment; operating without a sense of time; not requiring reasons or facts in knowing truth; experiencing intuition as leaps of insight; and recognizing the patterns of things in a holistic sense.

The non-verbal, intuitive gifts of the right brain cause fear in many people and most institutions mainly because they initially seem outside rational control. Yet, they are the soul of knowledge which, once they are welcomed, require the verbal and rational resources of the left brain to make them concrete and operative in our world. Either one without the other is incomplete. The right brain without the left can be formless chaos; the left without the right an empty shell, devoid of soul. This last statement echoes many cries from members of our churches for whom the spirit has gone from our institutions.

How then, do we as facilitators of adult religious education weave together the whole experience? There are at least five principles that guide our use of right-brain activities in learning experiences.[4] These are:

1. Relaxation is of primary importance. A good way to help people relax is by taking time to breathe deeply and slowly, and/or to engage in one of the forms of muscle relaxation readily available.

2. Attend to the environment of the room so that, as far as possible, the setting (chairs, warmth, space arrangement) is comfortable for the learners. Make an effort to remove external distractions, and if there is one (for example, the outside noise of street cleaning) which cannot be removed, invite learners to notice it and then let it go.

3. Right-brain learning is play. There is no right way or wrong way of doing it. Gradually, people lose their fear of right-brain learning by being relieved of this need to know the right way to do it. In this way, right-brain learning develops the person's ability to know and trust her or his own experience.

4. Using right brain activities enables people to turn off their rational thought patterns and try a fresh approach to their topic. For example, invite participants to

talk about the first thought that enters their minds when they hear the question, "What animal is an adult religious educator?" This opens up worlds of information on that topic that might never come forth in response to the assignment: "Define and describe an adult religious educator." And participants have fun, besides.

5. Right-brain learning is more about *being* than *doing*. Sometimes this calls forth the criticism that right-brain activity is a waste of time because nothing gets done, nothing gets fixed, no absolute answers emerge, and on and on. Somehow, these critics forget that doing and being enhance and enrich one another and are incomplete without each other. We notice that many important left-brain tasks get done without much of the struggle and fatigue if we have taken time to begin them with a right-brain activity.

Our experience as facilitators with a wide variety of groups, most of which are church-related, teaches us consistently that the best and longest-lasting work is done when we use a whole-brain approach to the learning experience.

Planning Methods

Maurice Taylor, in his chapter, has written some very practical recommendations for planning adult religious education experiences. In this section, we confine our remarks to only two aspects of planning: designing a learning event, and specifying helpful reflective techniques that distinguish clearly between reflection and evaluation.

Our model for designing a learning experience is an original one that applies the principles of adult learning as we have been discussing them so far—that is, a learning process that provides for all the learning styles that characterize a variety of participants. A lecture approach to learning could be one part of this experience, but it is not the principal approach we are using here. A format for using our model is provided at the end of this chapter.

Designing a learning experience begins immediately with a list of objectives for each of the activities a facilitator wants to include in the time allotted. For each objective, it is helpful to juxtapose the content relating to the objective.

The columns following the objective and the content help to ensure a balance in the interplay between the facilitator and the learners, one that specifies the action or input of the facilitator and another that lists the learner activity. If there is significantly more activity for the facilitator, for example, then it is easy to re-design in order to engage the learners in a more balanced way.

After this basic design is made, a further analysis of each segment is made, according to the Kolb[5] Learning Style Inventory. Is there something for each person according to her or his preferred way to learn? Does one style dominate, and how can that be changed, so that the event is more inclusive?

The next two columns invite the facilitator to list the handouts and the materials needed for each separate activity. Once this is completed, it is helpful to check the sequencing of the separate pieces and the time needed for each one. The purpose of this last element of the design is to enhance the dynamic flow or synergy of the whole experience, and to ensure a respect for boundaries of time.

Confusion often exists regarding the difference between reflection and evaluation of particular learning experiences. A clarification that many people find helpful is simply this: evaluation is always related to the objectives and to them alone. How well have they been achieved? Reflection, on the other hand, gives ways for the learners to connect themselves to the learning experience, ways that enable more conscious integration on the part of the learners. Using reflective techniques after a learning experience is a way to enhance the learning; we believe that learning is enriched when the experience is attended to—that is, when we become aware of what we have learned. Some examples of reflection questions follow.

1. *General questions:* What did you learn that you wanted to? What did you learn that was a surprise? What did you learn that you didn't want to?
2. *Open-ended statements:* I'm going to start...I'm going to stop...I'm going to continue...
3. *For a longer learning event, a series such as:* For you, who or what were the significant people...activities or projects...prayer times...groups...events or happenings...dreams...specific experiences or insights...decisions...that have importance for you?

Reflection questions are not examination questions. Their only intention is to put the learner in touch with what is inside their new perceptions; to probe, to own the learning that she or he has experienced.

Establishing a Learning Climate

The word climate as it relates to learning includes the concept of environment, and is larger than the usual meaning of that word. For this reason, we often use the term climate/environment in our work. We define climate/ environment as a network of messages that are communicated from the physical surroundings, human and interpersonal relations, and the organizational setting. These messages are directed primarily to feelings and emotions. Establishing a learning climate, then, requires attention to each of the levels of physical surroundings, the human and interpersonal relations, and to the organizational setting.

Arranging the *physical surroundings* to facilitate the adult learning experience means paying attention to such necessary things as: the temperature of the room; whether there is adequate lighting; whether the chairs are comfortable; whether charts can be seen; and whether the room arrangement is flexible enough for the needs of the group. Claiming the room for and with the group gives the message that the facilitator cares about what happens to the participants and invites them to do the same. It also models a respect for the fact that physical comfort contributes to the adult learning experience.

There are also some concrete ways in which *human and interpersonal relations* can be honored in establishing a learning climate. For example, the facilitator is careful to have completed her or his preparations before the event begins, so that a warm welcome can be extended to every participant. She or he has already arranged the room so it, too, is welcoming; chairs arranged without rigidity; no power station (lectern or table in a prominent place) announcing the facilitator's authority. During the learning event, the facilitator engages the learners as much as possible in mutual planning; this affirms their important place in the experience. One cardinal principle of adult learning that enhances this level of the learning climate is that of ending on time. Even if the facilitator has not begun at the precise moment scheduled, ending at the previously agreed time greatly promotes interpersonal relations in any learning event.

Finally, the *organizational setting* contributes significantly to establishing a learning climate. Prior communications (announcements of meeting times, the literature connected with the event) speak clearly to prospective participants about the quality of what is to come. Posting the agenda for the whole learning experience as well as for each segment, and being clear on closing times, indicates to participants the willingness of the facilitator to be accountable to them.

All of these messages speak to the feelings and emotions of adult learners. We hope that our messages convey to them that they are respected and that they have a significant part to play, along with the facilitator, in their own learning.

Communicating Effectively

As basic as effective communication is to preparing to be an adult religious educator, we cannot assume that this important area will be given the value it requires. Thus, we mention it briefly here in two of its dimensions. Active listening and clarity of thought and speech are two anchor points for improving one's communication skills in an ongoing way.

Active listening involves paying attention to the other with the whole self. We hear not only with our ears, but with our eyes, our minds, our bodies, and our hearts. We give verbal and non-verbal feedback when we are engaged in active listening. Our communication is fifty-five percent non-verbal, thirty-eight percent inflection and tone, and only seven percent in words. Attending to our non-verbal messages in communicating, then, carries the same significance as knowing our assumptions—they both increase our possibility for being more effective adult religious educators.

Clarity of thought and speech is a skill that can be improved with practice. Acknowledging that the language of adult religious education need not elicit a common understanding with our adult learners, and respectfully noticing that people often interpret words differently according to personal experience, we are challenged to the discipline of knowing clearly what we mean and of being ready to dialogue about it.

In the area of effective communication, the importance of the ongoing practice of both active listening and clarifying thought and speech cannot be over-emphasized. As we have mentioned in other areas, the presence of good communications theory abounds; it is often the practice of it that is neglected. Given our multilevel approach to preparing for facilitating adult religious education, we hold out *active listening* and the *willingness to clarify thought and speech* as foundational to our practice.

Managing Conflict

In an earlier section we referred to the importance of openly acknowledging the feelings of group members, and of finding ways to work with them. Managing conflict is one of the significant skills that facilitates the work of adult religious education; avoiding or denying conflict is a sure way to undermine the best work a facilitator is capable of doing.

All the dimensions of preparing to facilitate adult religious education discussed thus far in this chapter contribute to successful management of conflict. Knowing one's assumptions, balancing inner/outer processes, respecting differences, recognizing that people learn differently, clarifying one's own thought and speech—all of these make a stable foundation for the inevitable moments of conflict that arise in healthy group situations. Healthy, yes, because conflict can be creative and tension can be productive. They are faces of an energy that can enhance the dynamic growth of an adult learning experience. Specific skills contribute to managing conflict productively. The A, B, Cs of these skills are:

A. *Understanding conflict* by clarifying and defining problems before getting involved;
B. Learning to look for the *growth opportunities* that are often hidden in conflict circumstances;
C. *Recognizing the differences* causing this particular conflict and sorting out the emotional landscapes involved;
D. Learning to *minimize the effect* of negative and hostile behavior;
E. Dealing openly with any *gender issues* that are present;
F. Learning and practising the *special communicating skills* appropriate to conflict situations; and
G. *Caring for oneself* during conflict experiences.

We believe that practising conflict management skills in one's own life and work enhances the quality of facilitating adult religious education. Conflict management frees the energy at the source of conflict; engages the opinions of all adult learners rather than of a few, and benefits everyone from the gifts of all members of a faith community.

CONTENT

As we stated earlier in this chapter, it is our belief that the content of adult religious education cannot stand in a vacuum. It is highly influenced by the persons involved in the learning situation—that is, the learner herself or himself, the adult religious educator, and the group which is learning together. In this section we wish to point out two further aspects of content: the context which is described in more detail in Margaret Fisher Brillinger's chapter and the preparation for content.

Contextualizing content means asking the question, "How does this concept or information fit the broader picture, and how does it relate to the learners' living experience?" The context changes, then, in two directions. The Exodus story, for example, would be different as a source of adult learning in Peru than it would be in Canada; different in a Baptist context than it would be in an Anglican parish; different in a class of graduate students than it would be in a class of beginners with no knowledge of scripture. In addition, the context in which the story itself was written is important knowledge in order to know how it was intended in its origins. Context, then, is multilayered, and every dimension of it is significant for the learner, because content does not stand alone. Attending to the contextual layers of content reveals its nature and purpose in ways that invite the learner to a deeper integration of the content itself. For this reason, contextualizing content is an important facet of preparation work for the adult religious educator.

One of the tasks of immediate preparation for a learning experience is a clear understanding of who is responsible for content. According to the principles inherent in this chapter, content is not always the sole responsibility of the adult religious educator; sometimes it comes from the learners themselves and sometimes it is a shared responsibility. In some cases, it is even possible for an adult religious educator to facilitate learning in an area of knowledge that he or she is not familiar with, if a clear understanding of facilitation skills is operative.

We wish to emphasize here, as we draw this chapter to a close, that we believe the most important element in the learning situation is the learner, not the content. To facilitate learning from the opposite stance—for example, that the content is more important than the learner—is to perpetuate what has been called the *scarcity model* of education. In this model, one person has all the necessary knowledge and others do not; the person who has the information is powerful and the others are not. This understanding of adult learning directly undermines the important contribution made by every adult in any learning situation. It effectively negates the approach to adult learning that we have outlined in this chapter.

FROM PREPARATION FOR FACILITATION TO SELECTION OF APPROPRIATE RESOURCES

We have said again and again that at the heart of adult religious education is the person of the adult religious educator. If preparation does not happen in the life of the facilitator, in her or his heart as well as intellect, then all the other levels are empty. The interactive techniques that the adult religious educator uses flow from the person and are congruent with her or his unique approach. These dimensions—the person of the adult religious educator and the interactive techniques—are then in dialogue with the adult learners themselves, and the content of the learning event is contextualized by the particular circumstances of the learners and the world at any given moment. The content is enriched from the inside outward, and not in the opposite direction. Finally, the model we have chosen to illustrate key elements of preparation for the adult religious educator shows the permeable boundaries that divide each dimension, conveying the flow of each with the other in a fluid way.

The work of adult religious education is a vocation in our most traditional sense of that word. It is a way of life, an attitude, not a job to be done in certain hours and then left behind at other times. Preparation for this work is the experience of living and an ongoing commitment to learning and to sharing learning with other adults. Understood and lived in this way, preparing for the work of adult religious education in itself facilitates the community of faith and brings about the reign of God in our universe.

DISCUSSION QUESTIONS

These questions can be used as a guide in preparing yourself as a facilitator of adults in any religious education setting. In using them, you will be able to link the material in the chapter to your own situation. Each question could form the basis of a study session, either alone or with other facilitators.

1. Make a list of your assumptions as a facilitator in the specific context in which you find yourself. Your list will include your assumptions about the learners, about religious education and learning, about your role, about the church and learning, about the topic of your session.

2. Analyze a recent session you facilitated—or the plans of an upcoming session—using the Kolb[5] Learning Cycle. Where did you call on or involve the learners' experience? Where were the learners reflecting on their experience? Where were they enabled to connect their experience and reflections to a concept of theory? And where were they facilitated to apply their learning in a new experience?

3. Think of your next session with adult learners. Design an opening question relating to your topic that will guarantee success for the learners, affirming their

personal experience and yet not be simplistic or condescending.

4. Examine the list of basic processes for learning in this chapter. Which one do you always facilitate well? List the things you do that initiate this process in the learners. Which process is least attended to by you, the facilitator? What concrete things can you do to develop this process in the learners?

5. Make a list of the non-verbal messages you want to send to the learners in the sessions you facilitate. What can you do to ensure that these non-verbal messages are directed to their feelings and emotions?

6. What strengths do you have in dealing with conflict? How can you nurture and increase these strengths? What prevents you from dealing with conflict successfully? What can you do to minimize or eradicate these difficulties?

NOTES

1. Gerald Pine and Peter Horne, "Principles and Conditions of Adult Learning," *Adult Leadership* (Spring, 1969). The article outlines practical ways to use the principles of adult learning and to establish optimal conditions for that learning.

2. See David A. Kolb, Irwin M. Rubin, and James M. McIntrye, *Organizational Psychology: A Book of Readings*, 2nd Ed. (Englewood Cliffs, N.J.: Prentice-Hall, 1974).

3. Virginia Griffin, Associate Professor, Department of Adult Education, The Ontario Institute for Studies in Education, Toronto, Canada.

4. Kolb, Rubin, and McIntrye, *Organizational Psychology*.

5. Marge Denis with Caryl Green, "Facilitating Right Brain Learning," *Caravan*, 2, no. 6 (Spring, 1988).

6. Kolb, Rubin, and McIntrye, *Organizational Psychology*.

ABOUT THE AUTHORS

Marge Denis, Director of Margaret Denis and Associates Limited, has been an adult educator in various capacities for over twenty-five years. With a doctorate in Adult Education from The Ontario Institute for Studies in Education, she has been an Associate Professor in the Department of Adult Education as well as Associate Professor in the Toronto School of Theology. Her doctoral research focused on an original investigation of intuitive learning among adults. Marge has served on the National Advisory Committee on Adult Religious Education for the Canadian Catholic Conference of Bishops. She has developed a program, Developing Facilitation Skills, which has been offered to persons in ministry in over ten centers in Canada, the United States and Australia.

Brenda Peddigrew is a Sister of Mercy of Newfoundland and presently is working as a full-time associate with Margaret Denis and Associates. Brenda's twenty-seven years of experience in education includes teaching at the high school and adult level as well as extensive experience in Adult Faith Development, both locally and nationally. As well, Brenda has served on the National Advisory Committee on Adult Religious Education for the Canadian Catholic Conference of Bishops. She facilitates process for a variety of groups, including women's spirituality, and is a free-lance poet and writer.

PLANNING DESIGN WORKSHEET

Time	Objectives	Content	Action/Input (Facilitator)	Learner Activity	Learning Styles	Handouts	Materials Needed
S							
E							
Q							
U							
E							
N							
C							
I							
N							
G							

2. RESOURCES FOR ADULT RELIGIOUS EDUCATION

R. E. Y. Wickett and M. L. Freitag

Any journey requires provisions that will sustain the traveller. A faith journey is sustained by many things, including the process of learning. Faith development involves a journey that requires learning and relevant resources to sustain it. This chapter examines the resources which sustain the faith journey of the adult learner.

Throughout history, religious educators have relied on primary resources of textual and oral origins for use in the education and support of individuals and communities in their journeys of faith development. There has been an introduction of new technologies in educational and religious thought within the last century, all of which have had an impact on the type, variety and use of resources in contemporary adult religious education.

Society is breaking away from traditional concepts of religion, while education has become learner-focused and pedagogically varied. This situation has placed the adult religious educator in an environment characterized by change and diversity. These changes have created a scenario of exciting challenge and possibility for the adult religious educator. In the area of resources for adult religious education, technological and educational diversity can enhance the educational experience due to the wide ranging possibilities of resource types and their potential applications to the variety of religious educational endeavors.

Traditional resource bases are being supplemented by new technologies which have allowed access to a wealth of resources for use in modern educational directions. However, in order for educational resources to be used effectively to improve and support the practice of adult religious education, religious educators need to recognize the diverse and complex situations for learning which presently exist in society, and appropriately select and utilize resources from the variety of resources available.

Both the educator and the learner are faced with the issue of resource selection and use. Difficulties can arise within the learning process when selected resources are inappropriate to the educational content or model, or are inappropriate to the learner's abilities or experience. Both the educator and learner can work together to avoid these difficulties.

This chapter is concerned with the widest possible range of resources for the many purposes involving learning. Both human and material resources are included in its pages. The plethora of material necessitates an overview of the various types of resources instead of an in-depth review of specific resources. The human resources to be included are peers, educators, and community members. Material resources to be discussed include electronic, textual, and distance education.

Interwoven with the comments on the nature of resources are comments on the identification, selection, and use of resources that are required by the learner. The guidelines for resource development, selection, and use should assist the reader to make appropriate choices after a thorough search for the appropriate type of resource.

DEFINING RESOURCES

Like Cyril Houle, we use the term *resources* to include both humans and material which are external to the individual learner.[1] This does not deny the value of each individual's own personal experience, knowledge, skills, and values as resources to the learning process. As educators, we need to recognize the value of these internal resources while making efforts to provide those external resources which learners require.

Both Houle[2] and Malcolm Knowles[3] remind us that resources must be associated with other aspects of the process for learning. The greatest potential value of the resource may be in its use at the appropriate moment during the learning process.

External agencies are an important part of most adult learning experiences. Many agencies and individuals provide resources which can be used by a wide variety of learners in support of their learning activities. Many learners access these resources through courses and informal activities both inside as well as outside the faith community. However, learners have indicated that they require better resources to support their learning related to religious issues. The research by R. E. Y. Wickett[4] and by Wickett and G. Dunwoody[5] indicates the value of both human and material resources to many learners. Human resources may be divided into two groups, those people who provide content and those who provide support to the learning process. Material resources involve all non-human resources, including those which are electronic or non-electronic print based, those which present symbolic images of a non-print nature, such as pictures, films, videos, or any interaction with a non-human resource. Certain resources are used to communicate the content which is to be learned. For example, a book may contain the new knowledge that someone wishes to acquire. Other resources are used to stimulate individual thought or to guide discussion within a group. A study guide is a good example of this type of resource.

An excellent categorization of the nature of resources may be seen in Dale's cone of experience, which is described with additional comments by Knowles in *The Modern Practice of Adult Education: From Pedagogy to Andragogy*.[6] Dale sees the range of resources based upon the nature of the sensory experience which will occur when the learner interacts with the resource. The most abstract experience involves the resource which uses verbal symbols such as books, pamphlets, and so forth. The most concrete experience involves direct, real-life experience in some guided situation. It is suggested that readers consult Knowles' book because the original Dale reference is more difficult to obtain.

The Sources of Resources

Those who believe in a "Creator" have a specific view of the source of all resources on earth. This section refers to the sources from which the resources can be obtained directly from earthly sources by learners and educators.

There is no simple answer to the question, "where do resources come from?" Alan Thomas suggests that learning resources are an important issue for the public domain.[7] Because the issue of the spiritual or faith dimension is universal, public agencies such as libraries are involved in the supply of resources, along with religious institutions. No one has suggested that the separation of church and state implies the total absence of resources with any reference to a religious issue, but we know that religious and quasi-religious communities and organizations usually provide resources of different types in various forms.

The reality is that only religious communities and organizations are able to address many issues and concerns effectively. Our concern is that these communities do so in a way which is appropriate to their own principles as well as to the requirements of the learners who will use the resources.

FACTORS IN RESOURCE DECISION-MAKING

Decisions cannot be made about the resources for learning without reference to several key factors related to effectiveness and appropriateness. The learner's ability and commitment to use the resources are critical. The content to be learned is also important, as well as the nature of the educational model. The final factor is the educator who participates in the learning process with the learner.

Learners and Appropriate Resources

No decisions should be made about resources without specific reference to the learners who will use those resources.

We must consider the skills and abilities of the learners as well as the motivating factors for usage. An example of the necessary skills and abilities may be seen when a learner with a lower reading level is presented with resources designed for those with a higher reading level. We must ensure that resources are appropriate to the skills and abilities of the learner as well as the other requirements which he or she may have.

Some learners use resources to develop skills for specific forms of ministry. Others wish to learn in order to grow and change within themselves as persons, whereas still others learn in order to help to change the world in which they find themselves. Many learners enjoy learning for its own sake, and some enjoy the social context of learning; others prefer to explore new areas on their own.

An example which may illustrate how resources are affected by learner preferences may be found in programs for marital counseling. Some couples wishing to marry may choose to attend a premarital workshop where they can share their excitement, concerns, and learning experiences among other couples. However, other couples may wish for confidential counseling with their minister or other professional. Placing the "private" couple within a larger group setting may cause them anxiety and restrict their ability to participate in the program and utilize the resources which are meant to facilitate dialogue concerning their future together. Thus, while the content resources of premarital counseling may remain the same, the appropriate type, setting, and use of these resources can affect their benefit to the learner if the learner's needs are not attended to.

Our awareness of the multiplicity of learner styles, and the reasons for them, which may be found in various combinations, assist us not only in the choice of resources but also in suggestions for their utilization so that resources remain a beneficial tool for the learner's educational experience.

Content and Resources

In selecting resources it is important to ascertain the nature of the content to be learned in order to determine the nature of the resources to be used. Resources should contain all content to be learned at a level that is appropriate to the learner's level of comprehension.

The process of communication of content to the learner requires the use of an appropriate medium. For example, for a content area that involves skill development some use of human resources may be necessary. Other content, such as knowledge, may be communicated effectively in other ways, such as books or television.

Unemployment is currently a major concern for all of society, including the various faith communities. There are many support systems, retraining workshops, resumé writing and interview skills classes, and counseling services available for unemployed persons. For such programs, it may be possible to cover a portion of the content using electronic resources, such as instructional videos and books, but to rely solely on these resources omits important communications which occur with human resources. Through dialogue, resource people can be vital to the education of others about the human skills which are required for entering or reentering the work force, and they can personally address the learner's life changes and problems arising from unemployment.

With the content requirements of a program defined, it is important for the adult religious educator to support the selection of resources that will appropriately meet the content requirements. At the same time the educator must support the entire educational process for the learner.

Learning Models and Resources

The content of learning is processed through a learning model. The model itself can influence how content is expressed through resources. There are some resources which are appropriate within a wide range of learning models, whereas other resources are more limited in their application. Numerous models which support adult religious learning are described in books by Michael Galbraith,[8] Bruce Joyce and Marsha Weil,[9] and R.E.Y. Wickett.[10] The definition of the model which is used in this chapter is based on Wickett's definition of an educational model and is defined as follows: "A model will assist the educator to understand the nature of the learner's situation and to create a context in which the learner will be enabled to learn and grow through an appropriate process."[11]

As the model defines the overall process within which learning will occur, the selected resources must be consistent with the model chosen to facilitate the learning. Once model selection has occurred, decisions about specific procedures and resources must be consistent with the model.

An example of the need for consistency between resource and model may be seen in the models which are more learner directed. The *learner-centred* and the *learning covenant* models[12] illustrate this requirement. The selection of flexible resources is important in the process of these models in order to facilitate the learning. Flexible resources do not require the learner to learn everything in a manner dictated by the originator, but permit flexible entry points and self-direction. The choice of appropriate resources is central to the learning experience. Presenting a variety of resources within a learning environment is often beneficial because it permits individuality in the selection of resources suitable to a personal learning style.

Many adult religious education programs involve the traditional educational model of needs, objectives, strategies, implementation, and evaluation made popular by Knowles.[13] A variety of alternate models for adult religious education, including those mentioned in the previous paragraph, are described in *Models of Adult Religious Education Practice* by Wickett.[14] Each educational model has advantages and disadvantages and requires certain resources to be effective.

The Educator and Resources

The educator has a higher level of knowledge about available resources than most learners. He or she can identify, assist in the selection, supply or provide access, and assist in the usage of resources. This role of "facilitator" of resources use can be critical to the success of learning.

Librarians and other persons who maintain resource bases for access by learners soon discover the importance of their role to the learning process. There can be little doubt that these people play an educational role along with their responsibility to develop and maintain a particular resource base.

TYPES OF RESOURCES

Sensitivity to learner needs, and the awareness of content and model possibilities and limitations on resource selection aids the religious educator in determining how to select and utilize resources appropriately. However, because there are a plethora of resources from which to choose, it is equally vital that educators become aware of the types of resources available to improve their practice. Knowledge of human, material and electronic resources aid the practitioner in matching the available resources to program content, model, and learner needs.

People as Resources

Perhaps other people are the most important resources for many adult learners on their spiritual journey. Many people have experienced the support of others who share the same spiritual journey. This section discusses the roles of peers, educators, and the community-based persons who support learning.

The selection of human resources is important to the success of learning. When selecting and working with resource people, the following guidelines will apply:

1. Is the person and the content or process which she or he can supply appropriate for the learner? (a) Is the learner able to work effectively with the resource person? (b) Will the learner feel comfortable in working with the resource person?

2. Can the resource person provide the appropriate content or process? (a) Is the resource person the most appropriate for the transfer of content? (b) Is the resource person sufficiently flexible for the learner to focus on precisely what he or she needs to learn?

3. Is the resource person suitable for the context of the faith community in which they will be involved?

4. Is there an appropriate support system to ensure the proper use of the resource person if the learner is uncertain about any component?

Peer Resources

Before we refer to the role of the educator or community-based persons as human resources for learning, we should like to clarify the potential for relationships among the learners, whose journeys in faith often intersect or run parallel to each other. These learners can be immensely supportive of each other through their shared presence on the journey and through the opportunities for sharing perspectives and experiences.

Most adult educators have many memories of the contributions which group members have made in support of the learning of others. We have participated in and heard the stories of coffee break discussions or post-meeting sessions over a key issue. We know that others often share a perspective that informs where our own efforts have not been totally successful. There are times when peers challenge our views in ways which lead to new growth in faith.

Many sessions involve small group discussions in pairs or triads. Relationships are formed which provide a sense of cooperation and openness. These small groups provide a more intimate environment for a dialogue of faith, and may encourage contributions from those learners who are uncomfortable sharing in larger groups. For example, educational programs for single people, single parents, divorcees, or any group of people who share similar life experiences can profit from peer interaction. People who are in similar situations can benefit from the shared learning experience which can result from communication about their common circumstances. Such dialogue allows the learners to feel understood and less isolated, they can learn from each other in an environment of acceptance, and help each other to rebuild a sense of belonging. We must attempt to enable peer contributions to the learning process. They provide comfort, support, and enrich the process of learning through shared experience.

The Resource Role of the Educator

Perhaps the most important role for many adult religious educators is to learn how to be an enabler or facilitator of the learning process. This does not discount the potential for certain educators to provide content input in many situations. The statement merely reflects the view that most educators have considerably more knowledge in their respective content areas and relatively fewer skills in enabling the learner.

For those of us who are accustomed to preaching, lecturing, and other forms of one-way communication, the struggle to engage in two-way communications is not always as easy as it appears. Yet the research by Tough[15] and his colleagues, including work in religious learning by Wickett[16] and Wickett and Dunwoody,[17] tells us that we need to consider this issue of dialogue carefully in order to provide effective support to many learners. In areas of personal growth, such as the development of religious faith, "telling" people is not enough, no matter how well we may do it.

What learners need, in many instances, is support in creating a learning plan. They often require a resource person with a knowledge of human and material resources to assist them with access and choice of the resources. The educator, as facilitator, can then assist the learner to decide how and when to access appropriate resources.

The educator, in the role of the process facilitator, may need to assist the learner to access internal resources. We refer here to the learner's memories of experiences as well as those current experiences which are relevant to the learning process. We can assist through models and methods which enable reflection, prayer, meditation, and similar techniques. A nominal group process,[18] which is used in other areas of adult education, around a social issue such as AIDS, the environment, or poverty, may be quite useful here because it enables the learner to connect with both internal and external resources.

The most critical support for some learners is the knowledgeable, sympathetic listener who does not try to dominate the learning process but provides clarification, stimulation, and the support which a caring presence brings.[19] If we are committed to the learner's ability to respond to a call or vocation, as supportive educators we need to ensure that we do not dominate the means by which the learner responds to the call.

Community Resource Persons

When approaching the issue of human resources, it is important to note that the local community can often provide people who have assets and abilities which can be used to provide content for learning. Both faith communities and the secular community can provide resources for learning.

Religious education resources can often be accessed through local parishes or religious organizations. Clerical and lay resource persons may be available for issues in theology and liturgy. These resource persons may also contribute vocational experience in areas involving morality, alcoholism, retirement, and death and dying. Separate school boards may offer people who can provide information regarding religious education policies. If there is a seminary or religious college within the community, educators can access people from these institutions to speak on various religious concerns. Other valuable human resources which are often overlooked are the chaplains and/or other personnel from hospitals, care homes, outreach centers, family service centres, counseling agencies, and the prison systems. Who better to discuss an issue such as AIDS than someone from the community with direct knowledge of the health problem?

Examining the surrounding community for all the resources it provides allows the educator to expand and enrich the educational experience of the learner and educator alike. Human resources can expand educational programs to include special speakers, seminars, or workshops, and they can provide support for educational models in areas of individual learning.

Material Resources

This section refers to the resources that are not human. It is important to remember that certain material resources may be most effectively utilized when a human resource person is available to support the learner in using such materials appropriately for full benefit during the learning experience.

Material resources range from the "ancient" printed page to the latest in electronic technology. Such resources can be used individually or in cooperation with other material resources or with resource persons. They may be used in every possible situation from the formal classroom in an institutional setting to the privacy of the individual residence.

It would require several catalogues of materials to do justice to all the potential resource material in this area. As it is impossible to name all types of resources, please note that general guidelines for selection and use are indicated along with specific references to certain types.

The selection of material resources is a key to the success of many learning enterprises. Poor tools will inhibit the learner! When selecting, developing, and using materials, the following guidelines apply:

1. Are they appropriate for the learner? (a) Does the learner have the necessary skills to use the resource? (b) Will the learner feel comfortable in using the resource?

2. Does the resource contain the appropriate content? (a) Is the resource a suitable vehicle for the transfer of content? (b) Is the resource sufficiently flexible for the learner to focus on what he or she needs?

3. Are the resources suitable for the context of the faith community in which they will be used?

4. Is there an appropriate support system to ensure the proper use of the resources if the learner is uncertain about any component?

Electronic Resources

This is an exciting aspect for some learners, but we need to remember that others find it to be intimidating to the point of total inaction. We refer to both computers and other forms of electronic communication in this section.

Computer based technology has advanced tremendously over the past decade. It is now more accessible in terms of both cost and personal use than ever before. Many institutions such as public libraries, schools, and other community facilities are making it available to an ever-widening circle of people. We have both personal computers (PCs) and institutionally-based machines which enable us to have greater range and power at our disposal. It is possible to combine the PC and the institutionally-based machines through networks, thereby reducing the cost to the individual and maximizing our capacity to search for new information. Databases, which are simply electronic forms of libraries, can be entered through a vast, inter-connected electronic network.

Church magazines, such as *Church bytes*, enable us to learn more about computer resources and how to access them for ourselves and for the learners we serve. A new publication, *The Electric Mystics' Guide to the Internet*, is to be published soon by Scholars Press. This document will provide a directory of current "Electronic Documents, Online Conferences, Serials, Software, and Archives relevant to Religious Studies." This material is currently available on the internet via LISTSERV@ACADVM1. UOTTAWA.CA or LISTSERV@UOTTAWA as MYSTICSV1-TXT AND MYSTICSV3-TXT. Another useful volume of general information about the Internet is *The Whole Internet: User's Guide and Catalogue* by Ed Krol.[20]

Many educators need to learn how to access a wide range of electronic materials before assisting learners to do so. Many universities and public computer agencies frequently provide both entry-level and advanced computer training programs for the public. The reward of access to computer resources is a rich repository of information from all parts of our world.

Resources such as films, videotapes, and audiotapes provide an effective means of one-way electronic communication. When combined with other resources for discussion or designed in the interactive mode, they are a powerful stimulant to the process of learning. Excellent video presentations are available from many national and regional faith organizations. However, only larger faith groups usually have the financial and other needed resources to produce good quality video materials. It is necessary to present high quality video materials to the learners today because they live in a world of high quality video presentations.

One of the most effective means of assisting facilitators

of adult learning involves the use of video cameras and replay equipment to enable people to view themselves in a situation. This approach can be used in simulated or actual group activities. It includes videotaping the individual in action, then reviewing, and discussing the tape.

Videotaping allows the individuals to see and critique their own performance and to review and compare performance over time. They also have a basis for the consideration of feedback from others. One concern here is that people should not be too critical of themselves or of others. They need reinforcement regarding the positive aspects of the performance and positive encouragement regarding any negative aspect which should require improvement.

Textual Resources

We are all aware of the printed materials available in public libraries and bookstores. However, technological advances have enabled access to resources in faster, more efficient ways. University, seminary, and public libraries provide a vast selection of written texts, journals, and microfiche listings (also records, tapes, and videos). Many libraries provide computer *InfoAccess* terminals, which provide quick search abilities, as well as brief information synopsis of text contents. Interlibrary loans give access to materials from other libraries, locally, nationally, and internationally. For those libraries equipped with facsimile machines, journal articles can be received from other libraries for minimal fees. Some religious organizations and publishers of religious materials also offer mail-order book lists.

Resources often overlooked are those found within personal libraries. Educators often have personal access to a rich variety of books, theses, essays, journals, or newsletters which can be used to supplement and enrich educational content. Students are also often able to contribute their own resource material for shared use with other learners. Educator and student resources combine to establish variety in the type and amount of resources available for supporting the learning process.

Distance Education Resources

Advancement in the area of distance education has expanded the possibility and potential for more adults to participate in education by reducing barriers that previously prevented such opportunities. Adding to the tradition of public and private correspondence agencies, more recent utilization of various media vehicles such as television, radio, computers, satellites, and fibre optics have broadened the resource base for distance education, making this form of education a growth model for modern educational endeavors.

Numerous national and international faith groups are using distance education to assist the learning of their members. These resources are created and dispersed from central agencies which have the requisite financial capabilities. The focus of these resources vary from Bible studies to skills for ministry. Larger groups with more resources at their disposal may create and distribute resources which cannot be obtained through other means.

Distance education materials may be designed and used in both individual and group contexts. Individual learning may be necessary for certain content areas and for certain situations. If you have only one person in a faith community who wishes to learn some particular content and there are no local resources to provide sufficient support, a distance education approach using external resources will be needed. This need for external resources is also true for group situations.

The best distance education combines the appropriate communication of the content to be learned with a system or process for assimilation of the content, including support for the learner who has questions and concerns. Appropriate use of distance education resources must be governed by their coherence with the curriculum content and efficiency in meeting program objectives. The success of distance education programs is also strongly related to the type and amount of human resource supports available to the students. Content specialists and local support contacts should be available for telephone or personal liaison with the students throughout the program.

STIMULATING GROWTH FOR LEARNERS

Despite the vast amount and type of human and material resources which can be used to support adult religious learning, it is important to recognize that such resources are ineffective tools if they are not appropriately developed, selected, and used in relation to the process of learning. Both human and material resources are often applied within an environment which involves a wide variety of learners, learning styles, contents, contexts, and learning models.

Careful thought should be given to the choice and application of resources for each type of learning experience. The human resources to be considered should include the peer group, community resources, as well as the educator. The latter resource person should support the entire process and content component of learning.

A vast array of material resources may be considered. The growth of electronic resources via computers and other media presents both an opportunity and a challenge. Traditional textual resources such as books and news-letters continue to provide access to content. The growth of distance education materials should serve the learner who has limited access to other institutional resources.

The choice of resources depends upon their potential for effective use by the learner. Are they suitable in terms of the learner's abilities, background, and content require-ments? Is there a support system in place to ensure the use of the resource within the learning process? These ques-tions are appropriate for self-directed learning and for other-directed learning.

Appropriate use of material and human resources for adult religious learning can challenge, support, and stimulate growth for learners on their personal faith journeys. The educator's role, as the facilitator for the connection between the content to be learned and the learner, can be supportive and rewarding.

DISCUSSION QUESTIONS

1. What human and material resources could be used to facilitate:

(a) an independent learning project?

(b) a study group?

(c) a lay ministry program in a rural or urban parish?

2. What considerations are important in the selection and appropriate use of resources?

NOTES

1. Cyril O. Houle, *The Design of Education* (San Francisco: Jossey-Bass, 1972).

2. Ibid., p. 56.

3. Malcolm S. Knowles, *The Modern Practice of Adult Education: From Pedagogy to Andragogy*, rev. ed. (Chicago: Follett, 1980), p. 67.

4. R. E. Y. Wickett, "Adult Learning and Spiritual Growth," *Religious Education* 75, no.5 (July-August, 1980), pp. 452-461.

5. R. E. Y. Wickett and G. Dunwoody, "The Religious Learning of Catholic Adults in Early and Middle Adulthood," *Insight: A Journal of Adult Religious Education* 3, (1990), pp. 66-71.

6. Knowles, *The Modern Practice of Adult Education*, pp. 241-242.

7. Alan M. Thomas, *Beyond Education: A New Perspective on Society's Management of Learning* (San Francisco: Jossey-Bass, 1991), pp. 115-118.

8. Michael Galbraith, *Adult Learning Methods* (Malabar, Fl.: Kreiger, 1990).

9. Bruce Joyce and Marsha Weil, *Models of Teaching* (Englewood Cliffs, N.J.: Prentice-Hall, 1986).

10. R. E. Y. Wickett, *Models of Adult Religious Education Practice* (Birmingham, Ala.: Religious Education Press, 1991).

11. Ibid., p. 3.

12. Ibid., chapters 12 and 13.

13. Knowles, *The Modern Practice of Adult Education.*

14. Wickett, *Models of Adult Religious Education Practice.*

15. Allen M. Tough, *The Adult's Learning Projects: A Fresh Approach to Theory and Practice in Adult Learning,* 2nd ed. (Toronto, Ont.: The Ontario Institute for Studies in Education, 1979).

16. R. E. Y. Wickett, "Adult Learning and Spiritual Growth," pp. 452-462.

17. Wickett & Dunwoody, "The Religious Learning of Catholic Adults in Early and Middle Adulthood," pp. 66-71.

18. Galbraith, *Adult Learning Methods.*

19. Wickett, *Models of Adult Religious Education Practice,* pp. 93-99.

20. Ed Krol, *The Whole Internet: User's Guide and Catalogue* (Sebastopol, Calif.: O'Reilly and Associates, 1992).

ABOUT THE AUTHORS

R. E. Y. Wickett is a professor of adult and continuing education in the Department of Educational Foundations at the Universtiy of Saskatchewan. He teaches courses in adult learning and development and religious education.

Mary L. Freitag is a graduate student with interests in adult religious education. She is completing her master's degree and intends to pursue doctoral studies.

3. SELF-DIRECTED LEARNING
AS A NEW APPROACH

René Bédard

Educators concerned with people's ongoing spiritual development are looking for ways to improve daily practices in adult religious education in a significant way. New concepts like self-directed learning are appropriate for many adults who are seeking more responsibility for their religious education. Self-directed learning, because of its very different paradigm, can strengthen an adult's commitment to a stronger religious and spiritual practice. Self-directed learning as an approach to learning is more demanding, but the suitability of the approach for adult religious education is without doubt. It represents the richness of the Christian message. It is a way of transforming the way people live faith and of seeing themselves as partners in the ministry of the church.

Self-directed learning is a different way of looking at religious education; it is a new way for many adults. It is not so much the content that is new; rather, it is the way in which the process is carried out. An important point when introducing this approach is that both religious and spiritual growth should be viewed as the focal points. Often this new method provokes skepticism on the part of some people, but it must be kept in mind that the Christian invitation to grow spiritually is in perfect harmony with an adult's desire to take control of his or her own learning.

Traditionally, religious education has been the responsibility of institutions that were charged with spreading the Christian message. In general, people received the necessary instruction for religious and spiritual growth from competent authorities. However, they had to conform to the norms and rules imposed by the various denominations. This meant that within each Christian denomination an important network was established, so that each person shared the same beliefs, rites and functions. The same objectives and precepts were well articulated. Religious education was identical for all those who wanted to belong to the same religious grouping. These prescriptions reinforced the expert-directed approach to religious education.

In this chapter I discuss how a new approach to learning, called self-directed learning, has the potential to improve the practice of adult religious education. First, I point out certain reservations about this phenomenon which are grounded in past approaches to religious education. Second, I describe the impact this new learning approach has had in other educational fields and illustrate why I believe self-directed learning has an important role to play in religious education practice. I further explain how such an approach provides opportunities to promote both religious and spiritual experiences. Third, I conclude by discussing the richness of personal growth through self-directed learning and by pointing out why practitioners should be moving toward adopting this kind of learning approach.

THE ABSENCE OF SELF-DIRECTED LEARNING IN RELIGIOUS EDUCATION

Because most religious or Christian groupings are well organized and well structured institutions, church authorities over the years have carefully monitored the quality of the message that was being taught. Complex organizations were developed to spread the Christian message to the members of various denominations. All religious denominations jealously guarded their power and their authority. This provided them with exclusive authority with respect to the doctrines, mores and customs shared among members of their various communities. To control their members and to be assured that everything was well established, well respected, and faithfully obeyed, young Christians very early in life received religious instruction. In other words, the young Christian was taken charge of by his or her community. He or she subsequently referred to that community in all religious matters. This approach discouraged any efforts toward self-direction in religious learning.

The Ignorance and Fear about Self-Directed Learning

Religious education soon became a well guarded and well controlled territory. The hierarchy controlled all religious matters. Only the official magisterium was allowed to modify, alter, or even interpret the Christian message. A very specific casuistry was set up and theologians were then entrusted with explaining the different dimensions of the Christian message.

Christians who were raised in this context and highly conditioned by the omnipresence of an ecclesiastical establishment in all religious matters—whatever their age or social condition—were deprived of their responsibility for religious growth and for spiritual development. They were told what should be done and more specifically what should *not* be done. They were introduced to the different steps considered necessary for reaching the Christian ideal and, to the different models of that same ideal. They also were introduced to a whole set of rules and regulations that had to be followed. Personal freedom was ignored and individual initiative was not encouraged.

During this period, the emphasis in religious education was on developing dependent Christians. This approach was widely maintained by the different churches. It had as its intention the protecting of and the salvation of the faithful. It was viewed as a way for the faithful to have access to the kingdom of God. Religious learning was well defined, well planned, and well organized. Generally speaking, Christians submitted willingly to this type of religious education. They accepted, without question, almost all that was proposed by the official magisterium. A major characteristic of that time period was obedience to authority; Christians were led to believe that exterior agents would take care of their religious and moral education. Consequently, they became accustomed to accepting this type of authority. In this manner an attitude of docility was fostered.

It is unfortunate that most Christians, even today, have not been encouraged, in one way or another, to view religious education as one of their personal responsibilities. Marge Denis and Brenda Peddigrew point out in their chapter that adult religious education is a philosophy, an approach to learning, and a way of being. But somehow, Christians, at least in my view, have been left in ignorance regarding this fact. They were guided in the past by directives set forth in publications like *Le Cathéchisme des Provinces Écclésiastiques de Québec, Montréal et Ottawa* which admonished them with the following words: "It is in receiving the teaching of the Church through which God speaks, that we will know all that we should believe and practice."[1] Thus Christians abandoned themselves into the hands of religious authorities due to many irrational fears. More precisely, the fear of deviating, of going astray, of falling into error, or of questioning the compulsory norms have been powerful restraints which have led to personal irresponsibility.

What Are the Consequences of This Privation?

In all religious education matters, most Christians have been conditioned to blindly trust their pastors. While faithfully representing their institutions, pastors have unconsciously sought control of the religious behavior of their followers. As a result, Christians have relinquished any hold on the objectives, the means, and the resources of their religious education. They often perceived themselves as "beggars." Their Christian identity was seized, their moral individuality was denied, and their spiritual experience was ignored. This type of religious education produced a Christian outlook without perspective and without recourse. Unfortunately, masses of Christians blindly adopted this outlook. Very few exceptions were tolerated and those who dared to question the traditional model of religious education did so because that model did not correspond to the new realities of their lives and to their personal evolution as adults. Fortunately, as explained in the next section, new educational horizons have opened the way to fresh approaches to education and subsequently to different ways of looking at adult religious education.

THE IMPACT OF SELF-DIRECTED LEARNING IN MANY EDUCATIONAL FIELDS

Over the last few decades, the world of education has been introduced to new ways of acquiring knowledge. These new approaches attempt to answer, in a more comprehensive way, the dilemmas of a changing society. Traditional education can no longer cope with the many needs of adults who, for various reasons, return to studies, reorganize their careers, or are forced to retrain. Within this context, self-directed learning has taken root. As Malcolm Knowles explains, many adults want to

> take the initiative in diagnosing their learning needs, formulating learning goals, identifying human and material resources, choosing and implementing appropriate learning strategies, and evaluating learning outcomes.[2]

As a process, self-directed learning has opened many unexplored avenues for adult learners. Writers such as Huey Long and Associates, Huey Long and Redding, Gary Confessore and Huey Long[3] demonstrate that much research has been undertaken in this area. Theorists like Sharan Merriam and Rosemary Caffarella, Stephen Brookfield and Jack Mezirow[4] have sharpened and articulated the modalities of this approach in adult education. Some practitioners like Philip Candy and

George Piskurich[5] have pointed out the possible applications of self-directed learning in other disciplines and fields of practice. The enthusiasm generated by this concept has also encouraged scholars like René Bédard, Nicole Tremblay, and Carol Landry[6] to delineate the skills and attitudes learners need in order to undertake self-directed learning projects. As well, Ralph Brockett and Roger Hiemstra[7] have shown the inestimable value of self-directed learning in adult education by establishing the links between theory and practice.

The impact of self-directed learning in many educational fields is now well-known. For many adults, it is the first time they have had the opportunity to become responsible for their own learning. In the past they had been subject to institutional mandated curricula. However, self-directed learning views the adult learner from a very different vantage point. For example, Jack Mezirow explains that through self-directed learning an adult learner may discover many unexplored realities of his or her life.[8] In a similar vein, I have argued that the most precious right of the learner is the right to be oneself and to become what one wants to become.[9]

With the introduction of different learning methods many adults are better able to deal with various contextual settings. New social challenges, new professional environments, and new ways of understanding reality maximize the quality of learning. Philip Candy maintains that "all learners but particularly self-directed learners must be confronted with what to learn, how to approach learning tasks, in what order to tackle learning, how to understand or interpret new ideas, and how deeply to enter a subject."[10] Clarification of self-directed learning is still being sought;[11] but this fact aside, important vistas have opened up through this new approach and many adult learners are ready to explore them. Both quantitative and qualitative research findings note that the adult learners who have engaged in self-directed learning[12] have not been disappointed. Because their relationship to knowing is now more significant, more responsible, and more gratifying, they are better prepared to perceive themselves as *lifelong learners*.

THE IMPORTANCE OF SELF-DIRECTED
LEARNING IN ADULT RELIGIOUS EDUCATION

One of the first steps in promoting the importance of self-directed learning in adult religious education is to encourage religious educators to recognize the usefulness of the concept outside the academic domain. Self-directed learning as a learning phenomenon is not exclusive to academic fields only. For example, George Piskurich writes that "in the field of training and human resource development, particularly in technical and performance skills training, there are few tools as powerful, misunderstood, and misused as self-directed learning."[13] He makes a strong case for using a self-directed approach.

Certain religious educators also view self-directed learning as a novelty. At the beginning of this chapter, I noted that this approach to adult religious education is relatively unknown to many adults and for this reason some might be skeptical about its use. However, there are two positive dimensions to the self-directed learning approach that recommends its application in adult religious education: opportunities to promote religious experiences and opportunities to promote spiritual experiences.

Opportunities to Promote Religious Experiences

In the traditional context, religious experience has rarely kept pace with adult growth. Religious education, because of its institutional aspect, controlled to such a degree that almost no place was left for adult religious experience. Religious education was based on very defined beliefs. Because of its narrow perspective, religious education had a serious shortcoming—it failed to introduce the adult to a real and authentic religious experience.

Self-directed learning allows for what a traditional religious education has not permitted; the right and the privilege of adults to formulate personal objectives for true religious growth and to look for the means to fulfill those objectives. On this same point, R. Wickett and M. Freitag mention that the choice of appropriate resources to fulfill these objectives is central to the learning experience. In the past, however, Christian adults looked to the official magisterium for resources. They often believed and accepted their religious education without question. Nowadays, things are different. Adults question on many levels, and religious belief is no exception. By using a self-directed learning approach, the adult can explore the relationships that can take place between himself or herself and a supreme being. This same exploration can also take place between a Christian and a community of believers. What is important in religious education is not what is imposed from outside but what emerges from a person's inner being. In this process, the person takes into account her or his significant relationships with God and with other humans. The concept of religion is a very social one; it does not exist outside community. In my opinion, the misunderstanding of that concept has prevented many adults from questioning what was imposed from the outside that did not correspond to their personal development, their maturation, and their desire for religious experience.

It should not be forgotten that religious experience is a very personal experience; it is a lifelong journey. This path is usually chosen by those who want to grow and develop in the religious dimension of their lives. This is the reason why self-directed learning should be well understood by those who choose such an approach for their religious journey. It is an approach that requires a great deal of personal responsibility.

Instead of accepting predetermined beliefs in religious matters, the Christian adult should question himself or herself, look around, and expect to be confronted with new situations. He or she should not fear new beginnings, self-criticism and self-evaluation. Above all, the adult learner should respect his or her own growth even when this growth does not provide the satisfaction of having *the* truth. The adult learner must be convinced that religious growth will lead to personal truth. On this matter, Placide Gaboury maintains that what has been said or experienced by somebody other than yourself does not necessarily need to be verified by you to be true.[14]

The self-directed learner should also be aware of the process he or she is going through, even if it results in and creates limitations or requirements. To be capable of living a full and significant religious experience, a Christian needs to be self-determined. The institutional church is a very strong structure; it is not easy for people to question what theologians and the official magisterium have taken centuries to set up. Unfortunately, the reluctance to question has created people with many beliefs but with no faith.[15]

If the aim of religious education is to enter gradually into a relationship with a supreme being, rather than simply to adhere to a doctrine, self-directed learning is a very appropriate approach. In fact, self-directed learning allows Christians to distance themselves from the institutional church which often has created divisions between persons and nations. Only the self-directed adult can transcend norms, obligations, and rites. In so doing, he or she can feel better about what he or she needs in order to reach out to the supreme being. Dogmas, as they were originally conceived, understood, and taught were never intended for initiating personal religious experiences. On the contrary, they fostered an other-directed approach to what was viewed as a more pure and sincere faith. Finally, Christians espousing a self-directed approach will become more mature; they will come to realize it is from the inside and not the outside that the exigencies related to their objectives will appear; that is, the meeting of the Being will give meaning to their existence.

Adult Religious Education and Spiritual Experience

The aim of religious education is to gather believers around a doctrine that can be shared by respective denominations. Spiritual experience goes much further. It allows the adult to open up to oneself and to initiate a search whose parameters are dictated by the experience itself. Spiritual experience distances itself from many existing doctrines, such that the process for those who want to search, to discover, to go forward is not encapsulated in structures. Spiritual experience, by its own nature, suggests that it is important for adults to look inward so as to find all that will consolidate and strengthen the path to the infinite part of their being. Placide Gaboury says that "in the spiritual experience there are no dogmas nor revelations from above, we have to find ourselves by ourselves."[16]

In this type of process, self-directed learning can be viewed as a possible approach for those who feel restricted by religious institutions. Spiritual experience, through a self- directed approach, invites the adult to find for oneself the objectives of spiritual growth; it also allows the individual to select the best means to enter deeply into the discovery of "the one who accepts to walk inside himself or herself."[17] Self-directed learning permits one to look within for the resources that ensure that the spiritual journey will be real and authentic. As Marge Denis and Brenda Peddigrew explain in their chapter, this kind of learning is a deeply spiritual activity that honors the uniqueness of every learner.

Spiritual experience is not necessarily in opposition to religious education. Spiritual experience encompasses numerous perspectives; it guides adults to different paths which will free them from all that reduces their identity as believers. Spiritual experience requires a sound understanding of the various religious dimensions so that adult learners can question, criticize, and integrate these ideas into a more global vision of the world they are experiencing. Spiritual experience is much broader than religious experience, and because it is authentic, real and significant, it does not repudiate the past but tries to integrate it.

Only spiritual experience, can "re-grasp" religious dimensions and make them highly significant for adults who are searching for a different learning process. While religious education traditionally had as its aim the formation of submissive believers, spiritual experience requires a departure from known paths; it also demands a confrontation with the unknown and the infinite. In this confrontation, however, adults never abandon their religious growth, their evolution as believers, or their Christian development. Spiritual experience is the most refined form of religious education and the most significant journey of Christian education.

Because spiritual experience frees the believer, it gradually introduces the adult to realities unknown through religious education. In fact, all that emerges relating to the meaning of oneself in the universe is an integral part of a spiritual experience. As Jean Sullivan explains, "the one whose growth is interior because it is not the result of outside pressures"[18] is the one who has accepted to have faith in the experience he or she is now going through. In religious education, growth is often measured by the conformity to outside norms; "inside land" is not explored. It is only through authentic spiritual experience that one can discover this "inside land." It is also through this type of experience that the value of this "inside land" can be realized. Moreover, after this discovery, one will find in oneself the necessary means to nurture this territory and to remain comfortable in it. Fundamentally, it is through spiritual experience that spiritual freedom is established; it is through it that the freedom of people and nations also are established.[19] Religious education, on the contrary, attempts to confine people to doctrines whose foundations are mostly linked to terrestrial interests. Because spiritual experience speaks to the most authentic part of the person, it is toward this type of experience that the believer should aim if he or she wants to overcome the provincialism of conventional religions.[20]

THE RICHNESS OF PERSONAL GROWTH THROUGH SELF-DIRECTED LEARNING

I do not intend to argue here that religious growth is better served by self-directed learning than by other traditional approaches. However, it has been demonstrated by many writers and by the testimony of many witnesses that the religious growth of many believers has been limited by outside obstacles imposed by traditional approaches. As mentioned before, believers have been formed by doctrines that did not permit them to grow, to mature, and to be free spiritually. When some Christians begin to realize what they have become, they often confess with sorrow, that religion has made them something they are not. It is in that sense that Freud's works should be understood when he says that religion has kept man in infantilism.[21] Moreover, traditional religion has not been a vehicle for encouraging believers to look for their own truth. Here again, Freud's words appear appropriate; "if, to survive, a man cannot do without the religious illusion, this means that religion has poisoned him since childhood."[22]

It is spiritual experience that gives us back to ourselves. What belonged to us is given back: our freedom as children of God. Without that experience, levels of consciousness of our own spiritual growth cannot be attained. Spiritual experience allows for an entry into ourselves so that we can find out what we really are and what we really want to become. This can be done by experiencing carefully the movement of that ongoing experience. In the following text, one contemporary seeker described his own experience:

> Every time you enlarge that knowing—or acquire more of it—you see things in a different perspec-

tive. It isn't that it was really wrong before, but it's just seen quite differently, in a different light.... That's the essence of transformation, reaching the part of ourselves that knows, that doesn't feel threatened and doesn't fight the metamorphosis."[23]

Many people believe in the transformative power of spiritual experience. When Marilyn Ferguson speaks of the interior experience, she says:

Any experience bears results, any experience teaches us something. Whatever happens, we never lose because something is added to our understanding and to our competency. To discover is itself an experience."[24]

Abraham Maslow maintains that the value and the richness of experiences are to be found in a better integration of the dimensions of the person going through that process. When this is done,

the widening and enriching of consciousness through new perceptual experiences, many of which leave a lasting effect, is a little like improving the perceiver himself."[25]

In a book that introduces the way to God, Carl Jung says that spiritual experience is an experience of freedom because it allows us to abandon what was taught by worldly institutions that does not generate meaning.[26] Carl Rogers, too, explains that, if we open up to our own experience, and if we believe in it, we will get a better understanding of what we are now doing for our personal growth. This is the reason why he says:

The individual is becoming more able to listen to himself, to experience what is going on within himself.... He is more able fully to live the experiences of his organism rather than shutting them out of awareness."[27]

These are some of the conditions of our growth as believers. Christian growth cannot happen unless an awakening, even a brutal one, occurs that permits the person to feel responsible for the change. This responsibility, now synonymous with spiritual growth, takes place when adults get rid of all that is not meaningful and of all that enslaves them, especially in religious matters. Only then will they be capable of finding an interior life and putting aside spiritual underdevelopment.[28]

Self-directed learning is a powerful strategy for those who want to grow spiritually, because it allows for personal responsibility, because it takes into account personal learning style, and because it respects the learning characteristics of those who desire spiritual experience. Traditional religious education was restrictive; self-directed learning is rich and full of possibilities. Again, it is up to Christians themselves, through self-directed learning, to organize, plan, and delimit their spiritual search. If they want to be accompanied on their spiritual journey, it is again their responsibility to seek "wise people" to advise them, to enlighten them, or to guide them. The chapter by R. Wickett and M. Freitag discusses four guidelines when selecting and working with wise people. These practical suggestions seem appropriate here when speaking about an authentic spiritual search.

TOWARD A MORE SIGNIFICANT LEARNING EXPERIENCE

Self-directed learning in religious education and spiritual experience is not easy to embrace. When Christians undertake steps and actions that can provide a better religious education, they will need encouragement to move ahead in more significant ways, to find more gratifying approaches, and to search for more fulfilling experiences. Today, there are many signs that illustrate an estrangement from the religious message. Many religious leaders feel unprepared to cope with their responsibilities as Christian educators. This means that there is an urgency to create new ways for understanding the dimensions of the Christian message. All these new approaches should respect the believers' freedom with respect to the different manifestations of their spiritual search.

Two factors still keep us from embracing these approaches. First, ignorance of the fact that self-directed learning is the most mature form of all learning. A great deal of maturity is necessary before undertaking a journey into unknown and often complex territories. But we should never forget that the road of self-direction becomes clearer as we continue to follow it.[29] Second, the fear of making mistakes keeps many adults from exploring self-directed learning. They are afraid that marginality might be the price for daring to question and for discarding all that does not make a spiritual experience a significant one. Uncertainty is generally the necessary companion of all explorers,[30] including self-directed learners. Many adults unfortunately cannot cope with the burden of personal responsibility for that type of growth; this is unfortunate.

Self-directed learning is an exciting and stimulating approach to adult religious education because it surfaces doubts; it raises questions; and it sustains a learning process. Religious and spiritual domains cannot escape the exigency of self-directed learning because to grow religiously and spiritually has never meant accumulating certainties in all religious matters. It is the opposite that transforms. As Placide Gaboury profoundly states, people of faith like Job and Christ have, each in their own way, known that. From despair and doubt came the realization that this is the door that leads to faith. This means that only a freed knowledge can transcend fear, despair, and guilt.[31]

DISCUSSION QUESTIONS

1. What resources can I rely on in my religious education?

2. Do I always agree with what is proposed to me in religious education?

3. Am I afraid of the emerging religious dimensions in me that are not necessarily in line with the traditional religious institutions?

4. As members of a Christian community how can we identify resources that will guide us in our spiritual search?

5. How can these resources be used to enhance the Christian solidarity that should characterize our belonging to the church?

6. Do I feel capable of undertaking a spiritual search alone?

NOTES

1. *Le Catéchisme des Provinces Ecclésiastiques de Québec, Montréal et Ottawa* (Sherbrooke: Les éditions St-Raphaël, 1944), p. 2. Translation by René Bédard.

2. Malcolm, Knowles, *Self-Directed Learning, A Guide for Learners and Teachers* (Chicago: Follett 1975), p. 18.

3. See the works of Huey Long and Associates, *Advances in Research and Practice in Self-Directed Learning* (1990); Huey Long and Terrence Redding, *Self-Directed Learning Dissertation Abstracts* (1991); Gary Confessore and Huey Long, *Abstracts of Literature in Self-Directed Learning* 1966-1982. (1992) on *Self-Directed Learning*, all published by the Oklahoma Research Center for Continuing Professional and Higher Education of the University of Oklahoma, Norman, Oklahoma.

4. See the works of Sharan Merriam and Rosemary Caffarella, *Learning in Adulthood* (1991); Jack Mezirow, *Fostering Critical Reflection in Adulthood* (1990); Stephen Brookfield, *Understanding and Facilitating Adult Learning* (1986), all published in San Francisco, by Jossey-Bass.

5. See the works of Philip Candy, *Self-Direction for*

Lifelong Learning (1991), and George Piskurich, *Self-Directed Learning, a Practical Guide to Design, Development, and Implementation* (1993), published in San Francisco, by Jossey-Bass.

6. See the works of René Bédard, "Connaissance de Soi et Autonomie Personnelle: Deux Importants Préalables à l'Autodidaxie," *The Canadian Journal for the Study of Adult Education/La revue canadienne pour l'étude de l'éducation des adultes*, Vol. 3, no. 2, 1989, pp. 21-32; Nicole Tremblay, *Apprendre en Situation d'Autodidaxie* (Montréal: Les Presses de l'Université de Montréal, 1986); Carol Landry, *Les projets autodidactiques en éducation des adultes: fondements et interventions* (Rimouski: Université du Québec à Rimouski, monographie no. 31, 1986).

7. Ralph Brockett and Roger Hiemstra, "Bridging the Theory-Practice Gap in Self- Directed Learning," pp. 31-40, in *Self-Directed Learning: From Theory to Practice*, ed. Stephen Brookfield (San Francisco: Jossey-Bass, 1985), pp. 31-40.

8. Jack Mezirow and Associates, *Fostering Critical Reflection in Adulthood* (San Francisco: Jossey-Bass, 1990).

9. René Bédard, "Self-Directed Learning at the University Level: Yes, of course...in twenty five years," p. 3. (Paper presented at the *Seventh International Self-Directed Learning Symposium*, West Palm Beach, Fl. January 1993).

10. Philip Candy, *Self-Direction for Lifelong Learning* (San Francisco: Jossey-Bass, 1991), p. 280.

11. Sharan Merriam and Rosemary Caffarella, *Learning in Adulthood* (San Francisco: Jossey-Bass, 1991), p. 224.

12. Huey Long and Associates, *Self-Directed Learning: Application and Research* (Norman, Ok.: Oklahoma Research Center for Continuing and Higher Education, 1992).

13. George Piskurich, *Self-Directed Learning: A Practical Guide to Design, Development, and Implementation* (San Francisco: Jossey-Bass, 1993,), p. xi.

14. Placide Gaboury, *Une Voie Qui Demeure* (Montréal: Libre Expression, 1992), p. 43. Translation by René Bédard.

15. Ibid.

16. Ibid., p. 60.

17. Marie-Madeleine Davy, *L'Homme Intérieur et Ses Métamorphoses* (Paris: Epi, 1974), p. 30. Translation by René Bédard.

18. Jean Sulivan, *Parole du Passant* (Paris: Le Centurion, 1980), p. 116. Translation by René Bédard.

19. Ibid., p. 89.

20. Roger Savoie, *La Vipère et le Lion* (Montréal: Libre Expression, 1993), p. 177. Translation by René Bédard.

21. Sigmund Freud, "L'Avenir d'une Illusion," p. 31, in Olivier Reboul, "L'Adulte, Mythe ou Realité," Critère, no. 9, (Juin, 1973), pp. 87-122. Translation by René Bédard.

22. Ibid., p. 104.

23. Marilyn Ferguson, *The Aquarian Conspiracy: Personal and Social Transformation in the 1980s* (Los Angeles: J.P. Tarcher, 1980), p. 377.

24. Ibid., p. 107.

25. Abraham Maslow, *Religions, Values, and Peak Experiences* (New York: The Viking Press, 1972), p. 76.

26. Carl-Gustav Jung, "The Way to God," pp. 336-365, in Jolande Jacobi and R. F. C. Hull, *C. G. Jung: Psychological Reflections* (Princeton, N.J.: Princeton University Press, 1973).

27. Carl Rogers, *On Becoming a Person* (Boston: Houghton Mifflin Co., 1961), p. 188.

28. Jean Sulivan, *Parole du Passant* (Paris: Le Centurion, 1980), p. 54. Translation by René Bédard.

29. Marie-Madeleine Davy, *L'Homme Intérieur et Ses Métamorphoses* (Paris: Epi, 1974), p. 30. Translation by René Bédard.

30. Marilyn Ferguson, *The Aquarian Conspiracy*, p. 107.

31. Placide Gaboury, *Une voie qui demeure*, p. 44

ABOUT THE AUTHOR

René Bédard is full professor of Psychopedagogy and Adult Education at the University of Ottawa. He holds a masters degree in education and a Ph.D. in Psychopedagogy from the University of Ottawa. Adult psychology and adult learning are among the courses he gives at the graduate level. He is the advisor of many students at the M.A. and the Ph.D. levels and has written many articles on adult psychology and adult learning. He is a well-known lecturer at various school boards and presents many workshops on the psychological aspects of retirement to the civil servants who will soon retire from the public service.

4. ETHICS AND AUTHENTICITY: IMPLICATIONS FOR PRACTICE

Donald E. Smith

Ethics and authenticity, applied to adult religious education, means that we, as adult educators, participate in the development of the knowledge, skills, and attitudes of our adult learners, and that we attempt to perceive the world through their eyes. The driving force behind what is learned is not self-knowledge, not reality, but caring and service; our commitment as educators is to our adult learners. We are motivated to help them, to rejoice with them when they achieve their personal learning objectives, and to continue to help them when they do not. When we perform in this manner, we then are ethical and authentic adult educators; for without ethics and authenticity, there can be no truly effective adult religious education.

In this chapter, I speak from my experience as an adult educator within a federal bureaucracy and before that as a missionary religious educator in the Dominican Republic in the early and mid-sixties. Studying in Mexico in the spring of 1966, I also participated in a semester of learning activities with Ivan Illich, at that time a revolutionary missionary himself, who believed in the theory that "When you give people fish, you feed them for a day, but when you teach them how to fish, you feed them for a lifetime." Another one of his revolutionary ideas was that education was just another name for secular religion.

Not only have I been a practicing adult educator and learning manager for several large federal government departments for nearly thirty-five years, I have also had over thirty years of international experience facilitating the meaning, methods, measurement, and management

241

of adult learning activities. The texts quoted throughout this chapter not only are from authors in the academic environment, but include many references from the latest theories, principles, and practices in the field of organizational learning. A popular topic in organizational learning today is stewardship—a biblical term—which is now being used in many successful organizations. These organizations provide their adult employees with the opportunities and challenges to *learn how to learn.*

The ideas that I present are based on both my practical experiences and the published references. They are organized into four main themes: (a) ethics and authenticity as principles for learning; (b) learning from the inside to the outside; (c) stewardship as a new approach to adult education; and (d) the facilitative strategy of give more and you'll have more. Ways of applying these ideas are sprinkled throughout the chapter.

ETHICS AND AUTHENTICITY AS PRINCIPLES FOR LEARNING

Ethics and authenticity are two factors which I see as being closely related in an educational endeavor. Ethics involves the integrity of the educational endeavor, including that of the educator. Authenticity involves the genuineness of the endeavor, including that of the educator. I find it difficult to conceive of a person or an activity having integrity without being genuine, and vice versa.

Ethics

In his book *The Paradox of Success,* John R. O'Neill (1993) says that to be healthy and successful, any system—even an educational system—must include ethics (does it have integrity?), and aesthetics (is it pleasing and harmonious?).[1] A good bridge, he says, must have an ethical side of quality; that is, the right materials, engineering, and construction to make it strong. And a good bridge design must be aesthetically appealing or it will not last; it will be pulled down or allowed to fall down. Ethics and aesthetics, therefore, are the most important elements of building any system, but too often they are the last elements to be considered.

Aesthetics, like ethics, are often neglected in the frantic timetable of trying to achieve immediate success and satisfaction. When we put a lock on personal pleasure and turn away from emotion, says O'Neill, we have begun to corrupt the "aesthetic" self. At the same time, our system of ethics is damaged because the two are inextricably linked. So, when a person forgets how to care, or loses the ability to be emotionally honest, he or she also endangers the inner system of right and wrong; that is, the moral values which do not come about spontaneously. The latter must be learned, and more importantly, modelled.

Ethics means, therefore, that our consciousness enters into the mind of another, and that we perceive the world through those new eyes. We see ourselves not from within ourselves, but from within the center of another person. The driving force is not self-knowledge, not reality, but caring. Our devotion is to the person, the learner, as stated at the beginning of this chapter. This is true empathy: the ability to see ourselves as others see us, and to see them the way they wish to be seen.

When we make up our minds that we are indeed caring persons, that we want to be that kind of person, we become such persons. Without ethics, I believe there can be no true educational leadership, no real and lasting learning, no change nor growth, and no transformation.

Ethics, as integrity, morality, and principle, can be defined by reference to the concepts of equality, dignity, truthfulness, and liberty. Ethics mean a free commitment to justice and equality, to fairness. This aspect of being ethical often requires us to choose self-sacrifice willingly. Ethics as integrity means a commitment to the preservation of human dignity—the basis for adult religious education. It means that as an adult religious educator, I *do* what I *am*, and not the reverse.

The famous German theologian of the 1960s, 1970s, and 1980s, Hans Küng, wrote in his book *On Being A Christian* (1966) that "in ethics we shall not find the distinctive Christian feature in any abstract idea or in a principle, not simply in a special mentality, a background of meaning, a new disposition or motivation. And others too—Jews, Muslims, humanists of all types—can act out of 'love,' or in 'freedom,' in the light of a 'creation' or 'consummation.' The criterion of what is Christian, the distinctive Christian feature, is not an abstract something nor a Christ idea, not a Christology nor a Christocentric system of ideas; it is this concrete Jesus as the Christ, as the [a] standard."[2]

Authenticity as the Foundation of Trust

Authenticity, as I use it in this chapter, means a commitment to openness, truthfulness, and transparency which leads to trust. An open life is a simple life; we never need to remember the lies that we have told, nor bother to hide. Being open and sincere may be difficult at times, but overall it is the easiest of all. It is the most effective life, the life with the most warmly developed human connections. To be human is to need, and to be willing to receive—intimacy, bondedness, and connectedness.

Authenticity also means valuing and preserving liberty. Civilization journeys toward individualism, valuing the individual; that which requires respect for liberty as the supreme virtue. Happy persons are those who manage to live their lives in their own way. They think for themselves and are in charge of their own existence. They also learn more readily when they are happy and satisfied.

In short, to possess authenticity and practice ethical principles means to have made a choice, to be civilized. Through ethical behavior, we define the meaning of a civilized existence; no one else can do that for us. If you and I neglect ethical behavior, civilized behavior disappears. What is happening today in the Middle East and Bosnia demonstrates clearly what can happen when civilized behavior disappears. And yet, all sides claim to promulgate "religious" education. It appears, however, that the choice has also been made to be uncivilized.

In adult religious education, authenticity means integrity in products and services. A material product that is technologically-rich is also knowledge-rich, or information-rich. In addition, however, it must also be ethics-rich. It must not only satisfy our learners' material needs, but also address the needs of their inner and subjective side: their feelings and their attitudes. Adult religious education must not only have material content and knowledge content, but also must possess ethical content. That is the deeper meaning of quality. It is also the authenticity being practiced today by those organizations which are the most successful, profitable, and productive.

According to Peter Koestenbaum, in his excellent book entitled *Leadership: The Inner Side of Greatness* (1991), authenticity also means nobility. "Nobility of character, part of greatness in general, is also an ethical theme. Individual nobility, as demonstrated by the adult [religious] educator, may well be at the core of vision, realism, ethics, and courage. In education that is all expressed in the commitment to quality: being of service to another human [becoming], who in this case happens to be a learner."[3]

The Learning Principles

Ethics is a commitment to be of service. Although ethics drives education, to be ethical is to be motivated in a unique way; not by pleasure, fear, inclination, habit, approval, social pressure, or what is prudent. The source of our action is instead the rational fact that it is correct. This is to endorse neither dogmatism nor fanaticism; it is simply to say that to have character and authenticity is to act on the basis of what is morally right. The greatest ethicists and educators such as Socrates, the Stoics,

Spinoza, Kant, Mohammed, Christ, Buddha, and Gandhi
have taught us that.

Ethics in education means that our values give us
character. Socrates maintained that "the only way to harm
a man is to make him a worse man; virtue is knowledge;
and, no harm can come to a good man."[4] The final
strength of every human becoming is to preserve his or
her dignity, integrity and values—to protect the solid core.
Our identity is our authenticity; it is not our wealth nor
our teaching skills; only that which tarnishes our
authenticity does any significant harm to us.

Why be ethical? Is the reason because people feel
more comfortable with each other when they are ethical.
Actually, being ethical is a subjectively felt, fulfilling way
of being with others. Being ethical encourages the two
bases of mental health: presence and contact. Presence is
being fully present to ourselves and to others, and contact
is being fully in touch with our feelings and those of other
persons. Being ethical simplifies life. It makes life pure,
therefore, authentic. Ethics is based on trust, and trust is
based on trustworthiness. One can't have one without the
other.

Our authenticity as adult religious educators is our
decision to abide by the principles of equality, our
decision to respect the dignity of all human becomings
(our own included), our decision to be open and honest in
our relationships, and our decision to respect the liberty
of others and of ourselves. As long as we live by these
decisions, we possess authenticity. To do harm means to
choose no longer to live by these decisions.

Implications for Practice

Authenticity and ethics are considered to be the
foundation of what motivates most of our adult learners;
so how do we as adult educators win over the hearts and
minds of our learners? Koestenbaum presents a number
of ideas about motivation which can be applied in ethical
practice. I have abstracted a list of points from his work

and have adapted these points to the learning environment in general, and to adult religious education in particular. It is a list which I have incorporated into my facilitation of managerial, leadership, and learning activities. The way in which I use this list is to examine my planned learning activities against this list. I use it as a tool to test for the ethical validity of my practice. This list includes the following statements: (a) adult learners only motivate themselves; (b) true motivation arises from a sense of pride, honor, self-esteem, and self-worth; (c) the essence of pride can be enhanced through caring; (d) learners are motivated when they are noticed and heard; (e) acknowledgment must truly mean something; (f) recognition and rewards are signs of realistic learning acknowledgment; (g) a powerful motivational tool is faith, trust, and confidence in one's learners; (h) we must develop our adult learners, give them added value, make them better human becomings, and encourage them to become more interested in the journey of learning; (i) we must model, in every way we can, the authentic adult learner and leader in ourselves—our example is still the most effective motivator for our learners; (j) there is, however, an accountability side to motivation; some limits and expectations are (and should be) inflexible; (k) growth is a legitimate source of motivation, for growth is the nature of life itself; (l) we must announce that we will always distinguish clearly and sharply between effective learning and ineffective learning, and we must not be afraid to reach decisions accordingly.

Koestenbaum, claims that "authentic and ethical effectiveness equals influence (charisma, credibility, achievement) plus acknowledgement (recognition—making the learners feel important)."[6]

Part of this formula (ethical effectiveness = influence + acknowledgment) represents instructional technique, and part represents educational character. Both elements—technique and character—must be present in any learning intervention. Influence results from both personality and achievement. An adult religious educator possessing an authentic presence (one who has trust-worthiness and skill, with character) is so credible that validation from us as adult religious educators truly can mean something of value to all our learners.

In summary this first section contains a number of principles about ethics and authenticity. It also provides some practical suggestions for using the principles. In the next section I expand on the implications the principles have for educational practice.

THE LEARNING JOURNEY: FROM THE INSIDE TO THE OUTSIDE

Learning is like a journey. One begins from known points and references and forages into new ideas and perspectives. However, the transitions are not only in external features; many transitions are internal.

Learning Beyond Principles

The view we have of ourselves, according to Steven Covey in his remarkable and credible spiritual book *Principle-Centered Leadership* (1991), affects not only our attitudes and behaviors as adult religious educators, but also our views of other people. In fact, until we take into account how we see ourselves—and how we see others—we will be unable to understand how others see and feel about themselves and their world. Unaware, we will project our intentions on their behavior, and think ourselves to be objective. We then prescribe, instead of describe.

Learning from the inside out, according to Covey, is expressed in the following way: "If the vision we have of ourselves comes from the social mirror—from the opinions, perceptions, and paradigms of the people around us—our view of ourselves is like a reflection in the crazy mirror at the carnival. Specific data are disjointed and out of proportion. Such data are often more projection than reflection. They project the concerns and character weaknesses of people giving the input, rather than accurately reflecting what and who we are."[7]

When the basic source of our definition of ourselves is the social mirror, claims Covey, we may confuse the mirror reflection with our real self; in fact, we may begin to believe and accept the image in the mirror, even rejecting other, more positive views of ourselves unless they show the distortions we have come to accept.

One antidote for an inappropriate self-image is the affirmation of our worth and potential by another person. To affirm a person's worth and potential—one of our adult learners, for example—we may have to look at that person with the eye of faith, and treat him or her in terms of his or her potential, not his or her behavior. This isn't to say that we trust our learners unconditionally, but it does mean that we treat them respectfully, and trust them conditionally. It is an expression very close to what we mean today by the Pygmalion effect, or possibly the self-fulfilling prophecy.

Learning Begins With Self-Esteem

Some people say that you have to like yourself before you can like others. Erich Fromm states this as his thesis in his famous little book *The Art of Loving* (1956). However, "if we don't know ourselves, if we don't control ourselves, if we don't have mastery over ourselves, it's very hard to like ourselves, except in some superficial way."[8]

The place to begin building any relationship, according to Covey, is inside ourselves, inside our circle of influence, our own character. "As we become independent—proactive, centered in correct principles, value-driven, and able to organize and execute around the priorities in our life with integrity, we can choose to become interdependent—capable of building rich, enduring, and productive relationships with our [adult] learners."[9]

I re-read Leo Buscaglia's *Living, Loving, and Learning* (1982), in preparation for composing this chapter. The section that most relates to and confirms what I am saying here is where he states how much he loves the works of Martin Buber, and in particular Buber's concept of "I" and "Thou."[10] Buber teaches that each of us is a "Thou." When we're interacting with our adult learners, we must interact as if we are holy things, because we are indeed special. Unfortunately, according to Buber, we tend to interact with each other on the basis of "I" and "It."

As long, therefore, as we deal with our adult learners as "I" and "Thou," says Buber, we have dialogue. When we treat people as "I" and "It," it becomes monologue in our classes. As an adult religious educator, I do not want to talk to myself. I want to talk *to* you and *with* you. And I want *you* to talk with me. We both have dignity. We both have integrity. We both have ethical values.

Learners also have to learn that they won't be able to find themselves by looking outside themselves. They have to look inside—a similar conclusion to Covey's. It's not an easy trip, says Buscaglia, "the trip of finding one's uniqueness to share with others, because all of our lives we've been told by others who we are. It never occurs to us that we are already us. Most of us are what people tell us we are. Self-discovery, however, is like all discovery. It's never easy, but we can't count on others for insight. Ethical values and authenticity are not easy, but they are critical."[11]

Assisting Learners in Changing Their Meaning Perspectives

Adult religious educators are understandably concerned with the ethical implications of their efforts to assist learners in challenging and transforming their meaning perspectives. Jack Mezirow (1990) in his book *Fostering Critical Reflection in Adulthood* says that the essence of adult education consists of "helping adults construe experience in a way in which they will more clearly understand the reasons for their problems and the options open to them, so that they may assume responsibility for reaching and following through on their own decisions."[3]

Emancipatory education, explains Mezirow, helps learners become aware and critical of the presuppositions that shape their beliefs, but it is not the same thing as prescribing a preferred action to be taken. Our role as adult religious educators is to describe, not prescribe. Nor does the transformed meaning perspective itself prescribe the action to be taken; instead, it presents alternative rules, tactics, and criteria for judging. There are too many charlatans today who are ready to prescribe the "one best way" for us to achieve success, love, financial security, and even salvation.

Adult religious education becomes indoctrination or prescription when educators try to influence specific actions, or when they attempt to help learners to blindly follow the dictates of an unexamined set of culturally and religiously assimilated assumptions. It is better to show learners a new set of rules, tactics, and criteria that allows them to judge situations in which they must act for themselves. This description is significantly more effective as well as different from trying to engineer learners' consent in order for them to take the "solution" action prescribed by the adult religious educator.

This argument does not imply that educators should not hold nor model values. It is only natural to assume that our own meaning perspectives will be included among the alternative perspectives opened up for learners. I personally am not familiar with any educators, who take themselves seriously as educators, who would permit their own perspectives to be the only ones available to their learners, nor would they attempt to "sell" their own beliefs or consciously to foster dependency upon themselves. Most adult learners, in my religious and managerial experience, prefer to think for themselves. The implications for practice from this information are threefold: (a) model what you consider to be ethically appropriate activities and perspectives; (b) ensure that the learners are aware that your perspectives are only that, one of various alternatives; and (c) ensure that the learners are aware of other various alternatives. Often, an excellent way to do this is to get the learners themselves involved in proposing alternatives and in suggesting criteria for examining each alternative in comparison.

When I speak as an educator, I must recognize that each learner lives in a distinct world, and what we must do is discover what all our worlds have in common. A common refrain being used in today's large bureaucracies and learning institutions is: "We are all part of the problem; but are we all, equally, part of the solution."

Because we each experience ourselves to be the center, not only of our world but, from the point of view of direct experience, also of the whole world, each of us is indeed something unique and very special. Activities that encourage learners to contribute something from their unique perspectives also contribute to their willingness to examine other different perspectives. Similarly, from the hard-to-describe fact of individual-within-universal human experiences follows the concept of human dignity, self-esteem, and respect. These activities, and this concept, contribute to each person feeling the infinite value and worth of a single human "becoming." This attitude, in turn, is related to the concept of stewardship.

STEWARDSHIP—A NEW APPROACH TO ADULT EDUCATION

Stewardship is an old concept with new implications for adult educators. It involves three factors: the practice of stewardship, the right to choose, and learning from the spirit. In this section I provide practical points interspersed throughout the explanations.

The Practice of Stewardship

Stewardship, or service leadership, according to Peter Block and stated throughout his latest book *Stewardship* (1993), begins with the willingness to be accountable for some larger body other than ourselves—our community, our learners. This is an expression of the universality of education, as constantly maintained, practiced and taught by J. Roby Kidd when I was his student in 1976-79.

Stewardship springs from a set of beliefs and values about reforming our communities. It affirms our choice, as religious adult educators, for service toward our learners over the pursuit of self-interest. When we choose service over self-interest, we say that we are willing to be held deeply accountable without choosing to control the world and our learners around us. Service requires a level of trust that we are not used to holding. It is also based on the principles of ethics and authenticity.

Stewardship, true to its biblical meaning, is the choice for service. We serve best through partnership, rather than patriarchy. Dependency is the antithesis of stewardship, and so empowerment of adult learners becomes essential. But empowerment, I believe, is very similar to motivation. I, as educator, do not motivate my learners. I provide them, however, with the environment in which they can motivate themselves. Such is the case with empowerment. I do not empower learners. I provide them with the opportunity and tools in order for them to empower themselves.

For practical applications of this point, I draw upon Block.[13] He claims that four basic requirements need to be present in order for us, as religious educators, to promote empowerment which can result in a real partnership with adult learners: (a) each partner has to struggle with defining purpose, and then engage in dialogue with others about what we are trying to create. Partnership means that educator and learner are responsible for jointly defining vision and values—purpose gets defined through dialogue; (b) partners each have a right to say "no." Saying no is the fundamental way we have of differentiating ourselves. If we cannot say no, then saying yes has no meaning; (c) each person is responsible for outcomes in the learning situation—educators are no longer solely responsible for the morale, learning, or progress of their learners. If our learners want the freedom that partnership offers, the price of that freedom is to take personal accountability for the success and failure of their own learning. And, (d) in a partnership, not telling the truth to each other is generally considered as an act of betrayal—it is to be neither ethical nor authentic. Educators can examine their planned activities to see whether or to what degree these four requirements are indeed present, and to modify their planned activities, if appropriate, in order to increase the presence of these requirements.

The Right to Choose

We each have enormous ambivalence about our choices. We often don't want to choose between acting on our beliefs or our ambition. It is like saying that we really want to go to heaven, but we certainly do not want to die to get there! One way we avoid dealing with our own doubts as educators is by focusing on the doubts of our learners.

Conversations about empowerment always seem to turn to a discussion of how we, as educators, are going to change our adult learners. These outward glances at some point need to turn inward. Block, confirming even more the ideas of Covey and Koestenbaum, states: "Bringing our own spirituality into the learning environment is an inward journey. The revolution begins in our own hearts. It is the conversation about the ethics, authenticity, and integrity of our actions that ultimately gives us hope."[14]

There are several practical steps that we, as adult religious educators, can take to ensure that we maintain the possession and practice of ethics and authenticity when we are helping our adult learners learn. These are: (a) define a stewardship contract; (b) renegotiate control and personal accountability; (c) fully inform our learners; (d) create a desired learning future; (e) form learning teams; (f) change our learning management practices; (g) fit the learning architecture to the learning purpose; and

(h) redesign the reward and reinforcement systems. In other words, choose the appropriate path. These steps, again, can be carried out at any time by reviewing our planned activities in light of these suggestions.

Paraphrasing Block, one could say that adult learners have a right to their own stance and opinions, and even conclusions, but they do not have a right to refrain from entering into dialogue. A dialogue in learning based on ethics and authenticity between the educator and learner might look something like this:

- Seek and acknowledge the learner's positions.
- State our own choice for faith and commitment in the face of our own reservations.
- Invite the same choice from each learner.
- Implement the choice, but be willing to modify it, should that be necessary.

Adult learners need to be given time and support to make fundamental choices about faith and responsibility. The easy way out for the educator, according to Block, and one practiced by many bureaucratic managers and dogmatic facilitators is to "autocratically manage" the learning activity, and to tell the learners either to lead, to follow, or to get out of the way. But this is not the way of ethics and authenticity, nor is it the way of learning stewardship.

As adult religious educators, we are beginning our own voyage to discover a new world. We need to inform our learners what we are doing, we need the bankers to let us spend the money, but we do not need their sponsorship to manage the way we choose to spend it. All we need is our own willingness to begin the adventure and to live with the consequences. Living with consequences is demonstrable proof of our willingness to be ethical and authentic.

The ground of confidence for learning stewardship is that it provides a strategy which both serves the learning environment and honors our need to answer questions of safety, service, and freedom. It is summarized by Block in the following three statements:

(a) My security is discovered by experiencing my freedom and using it in service of something outside myself.

(b) I discover my freedom through the belief that my security lies within and is assured by acts of congruence and integrity, which are the essence of service.

(c) I can be of real service only when I take full responsibility for all my actions, which is the only safety I have, and when the choices I make are mine.[15]

An educator can use those three statements to reflect upon his or her practice. Service which is based on obligation is co-dependency and is a disguised form of control. Service that fully satisfies is done with no expectations of return, and is freely chosen, but above all, is applied in a caring way.

Learning from the Spirit

In a marvellous book, *Reawakening the Spirit in Work*, Jack Hawley (1993) maintains that one of the key roles of the (adult religious) educator is to teach about spirit, that aliveness which he considers is the real us.[16] Spirit, to Hawley, is the vitality that dwells in our body; it is our energy and zest. And spirit refers also to the very source of that energy which is at some level within us and is a part of us. Hawley, Koestenbaum, Buscaglia, Fromm, Mezirow, Covey, and Block say basically the same thing which is expressed by Hawley. Why should we, as adult educators, bother with this constant spiritual awareness? There are at least three answers, according to Hawley: (a) to get in step with ourselves; (b) to bring health; and (c) to attune to life's purpose.[17]

Our life direction, as we should teach it and—above all—demonstrate it, is to move into and become conscious of our constant spiritual awareness. That is the purpose of life—to live a life well-lived, a life of genuine satisfaction and peace—closer to home. Sooner or later when dealing with character and spirit, Hawley argues that we will run directly into the question of belief. Why? Because belief is the foundation, the bottom element of it. Belief is faith; belief is confidence and trust. Belief is not only the foundation of spirituality, but also it is the basis of character, learning, and community. Without basic belief, these structures will crumble, and so will learning.

Finally, then, what is the relationship between (a) spirit and (b) ethics and authenticity? Some writers sum them both up in one word: integrity. Therefore, what is integrity? Integrity, for the adult religious educator, is having the courage and self-discipline to live by our inner truths. There are five key ideas, according to Hawley, in this short definition of integrity: wholeness, goodness, courage, self-discipline, and living by inner truth.

Wholeness, he says, implies totality, soundness, perfection, and completeness—a sort of architectural structure of integrity and strength. Goodness completes the authenticity and ethics we think of when we use the term integrity. Included in goodness are human decency, fairness, kindness, politeness, and respect—an appropriate profile of an adult religious educator.

Courage, he continues, is not the absence of fear—in fact, it is proceeding in spite of fear. It is also telling the truth in the face of danger and embarrassment. It is finally going ahead and doing it or saying it even if it is uncomfortable. For most of us, learning has its anxious moments, as well as its moments of ecstasy.

Self-discipline is strengthening ourselves in accordance with our own inner promptings, maintains Hawley. It is also the cultivation of effective inner capabilities, and it involves the narrowing of one's attention so that it becomes a force that can be directed. It is the basis of self education, and "open" learning.

Finally, according to Hawley, living by our inner truth is possibly the most important of all. Inner truth communicates through faint whispers, thoughts, pictures, feelings, and aspirations buried deep within us. Each and every adult religious educator possesses this truth, and each of us has the capacity to call it forth. It is a learned skill and it requires time and effort—like any skill. It is a rediscovery of our subtle but true awareness.

In the appendix of his book, Hawley defines what he means by a *universal teacher*. He describes one Sai Baba from India, whom he considers a universal teacher, because Baba's spiritual message transcends the boundaries of any particular religion. Baba himself speaks of universality: "rain falling in different parts of the world flows through thousands of channels to reach the ocean... and so, too, religion and theologies, which all come from man's yearning for meaning; they too flow in a thousand ways, fertilizing many fields, refreshing tired people, and at last reach the Ocean."[18]

Baba's mission, like that of any religious educator, is to help his adult learners reach the ocean, whatever their background. He himself claims that his mission is "to help each of us to come home...and to live up to our divinity. Here I have glimpsed a way of living which, while challenging in the extreme, is richly rewarding...based on love, on service, on giving up material striving, and on forbearance and nonviolence in words and deeds, and peacefulness towards all."[19] In other words, through authenticity and ethics, practiced to their fullest, by way of descriptions, not prescriptions.

GIVE MORE AND YOU'LL HAVE MORE

Covey concludes his book on principles and practices by stating that the linking point between Sigmund Freud and Carl Jung involves conscience. Freud believed the conscience, or superego, was basically a social product. Jung believed it primarily to be part of the collective unconscious, transcending the mortal overlay of culture, race, religion, gender, or nationality. Covey believes that Jung was closer to the truth in his assessment.[20]

In working with many organizations that are continuously attempting to learn, as well as individuals who are also challenged to learn in helping them to prepare mission or value statements, Covey assumes that four conditions must be present, namely: (a) enough people; (b) who are interacting freely; (c) who are well-informed about the realities of their situation; and (d) who feel safe enough to express themselves without fear of censure, ridicule, or embarrassment.[21]

If this is the case, as it should be in each and every adult religious education class, then the values or principles and part of the mission statement all basically say the same thing, even though different words are used, regardless of nationality, culture, religion, or race. Education knows no frontiers, if it is founded on principles and practices of ethics and authenticity.

Further, according to Covey, the belief in a higher being is the true name and source of the collective unconscious and is, therefore, the ultimate moral authority in the universe—the foundation of ethics and authenticity. Believing in prayerful study of what our various prophets have taught us is the single most important and powerful discipline in life because it points our lives, like a compass, to the "true north"—our divine destiny.

One of Covey's professional and spiritual colleagues, Hyrum Smith, concludes his own powerful book *The 10 Natural Laws of Successful Time and Life Management* (1994) with a strategy intervention for facilitation.[22] This strategy for facilitation is part of his tenth law, which states, "Give more, and you'll have more." He refers to this as the adult religious educator possessing an abundance mentality.

For Smith, facilitating is more than just the simple sharing of knowledge. One of its other purposes is to bring about change, growth, and commitment to oneself and others in the lives of one's learners. "New knowledge is of little value if it doesn't change us, make us better individuals, and help us to be more productive, happy, and useful.... Teaching in the truest sense of the word, is

260 DONALD E. SMITH

energy transfer. It's a life force. A teacher whose own life is energized can transfer some of that energy to his students, and make them more fully alive. That is what motivating others is all about. It's a transfer—of knowledge, but more importantly, of energy."[23]

Adapting Covey's final paragraph in his book rather liberally, I conclude this chapter by challenging us so that our final epitaph as adult religious educators could read: "I want to be known as the [educator] who was thoroughly used up when I died, for the harder I worked the more I loved. I rejoiced in life for its own sake. Life was no brief candle to me; it was a sort of splendid torch which I had a hold of for the moment, and I wanted to make it burn as brightly as possible, before handing it on to future generations."[24]

DISCUSSION QUESTIONS

1. Based on your own past experiences, can you conclude that there really is a difference between education and religious education? What do these terms mean to you?

2. What is the true difference between spirituality and religiosity for you as an adult religious educator?

3. How important are the qualities of authenticity and ethics for you as an adult religious educator?

4. What accountability do you as an adult religious educator have in terms of what is learned in the classroom?

5. Can someone who does not practice what he or she preaches really be an effective (ethical and authentic) adult religious educator?

6. Do you as an adult religious educator have to possess an ecumenical spirit to be an effective religious educator?

NOTES

1. John R. O'Neill, *The Paradox of Success* (New York, New York: G.P. Putnam's Sons, 1993), p. 49.

2. Hans Küng, *On Being a Christian* (Garden City, N. Y.: Doubleday & Company, 1966), p. 549.

3. Peter Koestenbaum, *Leadership: The Inner Side of Greatness* (San Francisco: Jossey-Bass, 1991) p. 171. Here, I also wish to draw attention to J. Roby Kidd's usage of the word "becoming." It was one of his favorite expressions. By this term, he meant that all human beings are created equal and should be guaranteed equal opportunity.

4. Ibid., p. 174.

5. Ibid., p. 215.

6. Ibid., p. 215.

7. Steven Covey, *Principle-Centered Leadership* (New York: Summit Books, 1991), p. 57.

8. Erich Fromm, *The Art of Loving* (New York: Harper and Row, 1956), p. 57.

9. Covey, *Principle Centered Leadership*, p. 171.

10. Leo Buscaglia, *Living, Loving, and Learning* (New York: Holt, Rinehart and Winston, 1982), p. 192.

11. Ibid., p. 192.

12. Jack Mezirow, *Fostering Critical Reflection in Adulthood* (San Francisco: Jossey-Bass 1990), p. 361.

13. Peter Block, *Stewardship: Choosing Service Over Self-Interest* (San Francisco: Berrett-Koehler, 1993), p. 48.

14. Ibid., p. 48.

15. Ibid., p. 236.

16. Jack Hawley, *Reawakening the Spirit in Work* (San Francisco: Berrett- Koehler, 1993), p. 29.

17. Ibid., p. 29.

18. Ibid., p. 194.

19. Ibid., p. 194.

20. Covey, p. 323.

21. Covey, p. 323.

22. Hyrum W. Smith, *The 10 Natural Laws of Successful*

Time and Life Management (New York: Warner Books, 1994), p. 203.

23. Ibid., p. 203.

24. Covey, p. 324.

ABOUT THE AUTHOR

Donald E. Smith is currently Director, Future Learning, Transport Canada in Ottawa. He is also a faculty member of management and leadership education for the International Aviation Management Training Institute in Montreal, and co-partner in the Ottawa-based learning consulting firm "LEADERSHIP International." He has been a manager, educator and facilitator for nearly forty years, and since 1963 he has had the opportunity to work as an educator/learner in over twenty countries throughout the world. His undergraduate and graduate degrees were awarded to him from the State University of New York in Albany, and his doctorate in Adult Education from the University of Toronto in 1984.